Daughters of Lilith

Archer Lynch

Daughters of Lilith © 2010 by Donna Lynch & Steven Archer
All rights reserved

Published by Raw Dog Screaming Press
Bowie, MD

First Edition

Printed in the United States of America

ISBN 978-1-935738-08-4

www.RawDogScreaming.com

Daughters of Lilith

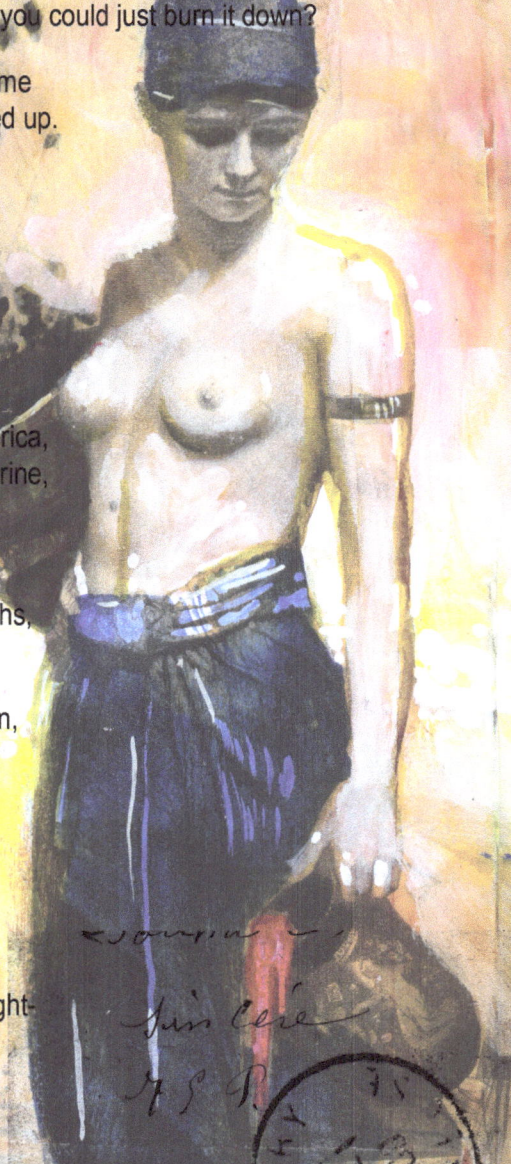

It's easy to pray in generalities. When you are sick, or someone you love dies, or you are afraid, or don't know how you'll pay your bills, it's simple to pray to whichever all-encompassing god you choose. But I find most deities, like greeting cards, to never be specific enough. The Loa in Voodoo come close, as do the saints and martyrs of the Catholic faith, but they are so old, I sometimes wonder if they can truly understand the trials and ills of their twenty-first century kin.

Who do you pray to when a lover betrays you, or you learn you can't carry a child?
Who do you call to when the only solace you know is in a bottle or a pill?
Or when you are feeling hateful and petty? Or when you look at the hubris of the crowded, polluted world around you and, for better or worse, wish you could just burn it down?

And right on cue, as though one of us had whispered some anachronistic incantation- that was when the girls showed up.

One by one, they came to us.
Some of them came in with early spring winds, those little girls with ribbons and more worldly insight than any child should ever have. Some came slinking in amidst packs of wolves, lion prides and skulks of foxes. Some were ripped through the veil, while others were born and born again of rage and fire and pain and loss. Some found us in the forests, the swamps of South America, and in the jungle. So many arrived smelling of salt and brine, and a few even accompanied me home from bars.

But they all came, showing themselves, speaking their names to Steven, and telling the tales of their lives, deaths, and rebirths to me.

And when it was done, these beautiful monsters, children, serpents, killers, lovers, and mothers became our new saints and sisters. And, as we would quickly learn, they were also the daughters of the original libertine –the first beautiful monster- Lilith.

I pray we've done them justice. I pray they know how they may have saved me. And I pray that if you ever don't know where to turn -because nothing feels quite right- you might remember this and pray to them.

-Donna Lynch
April 2010

Sister slicer

Little girls who cry in fright
At every creature of the night
May find that they are unaware
Of dangers lurking in the light

But little girls who play with knives
Have sharper wits and sharper eyes
They know that men and sheep alike
Are sometimes wolves in sweet disguise

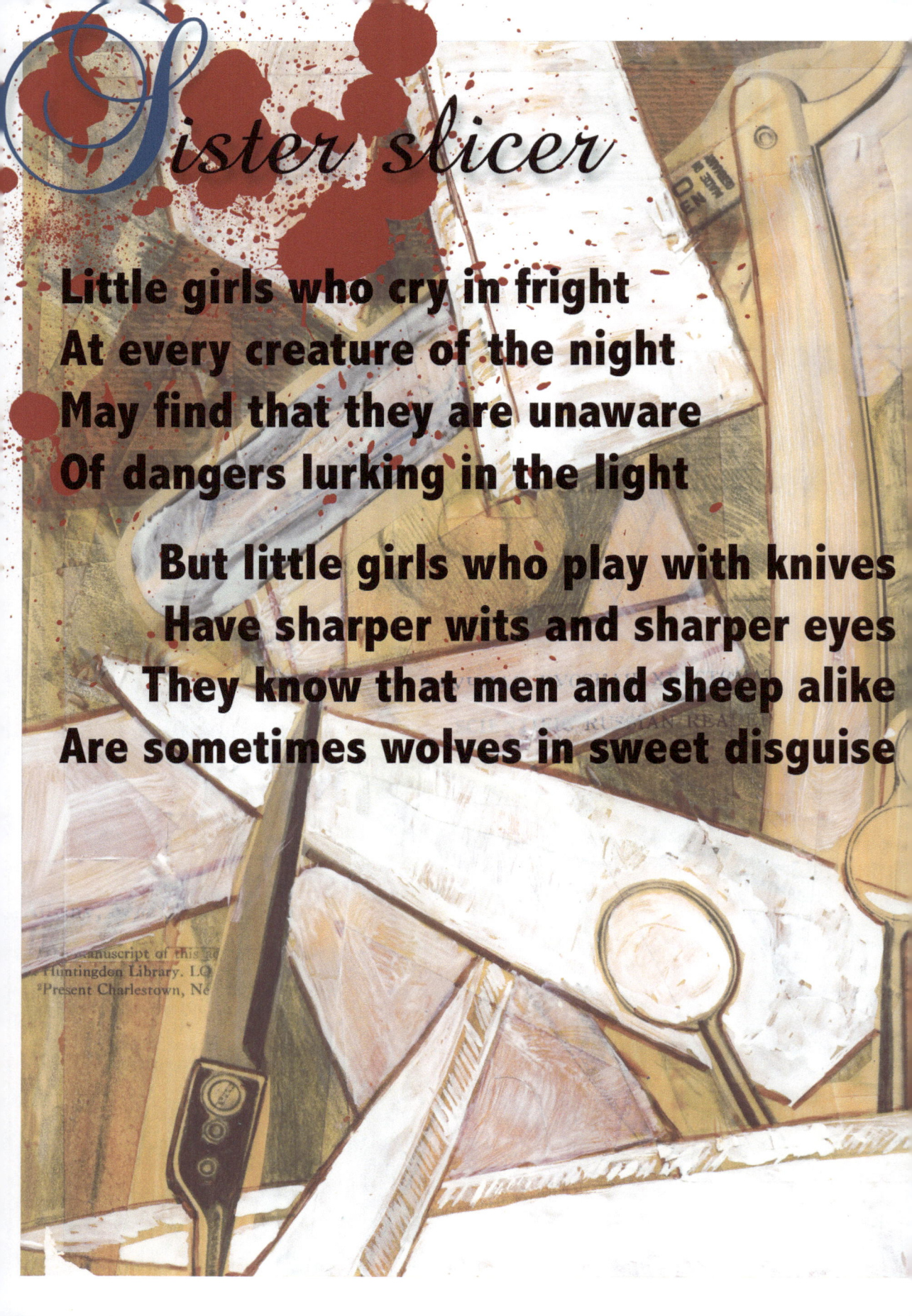

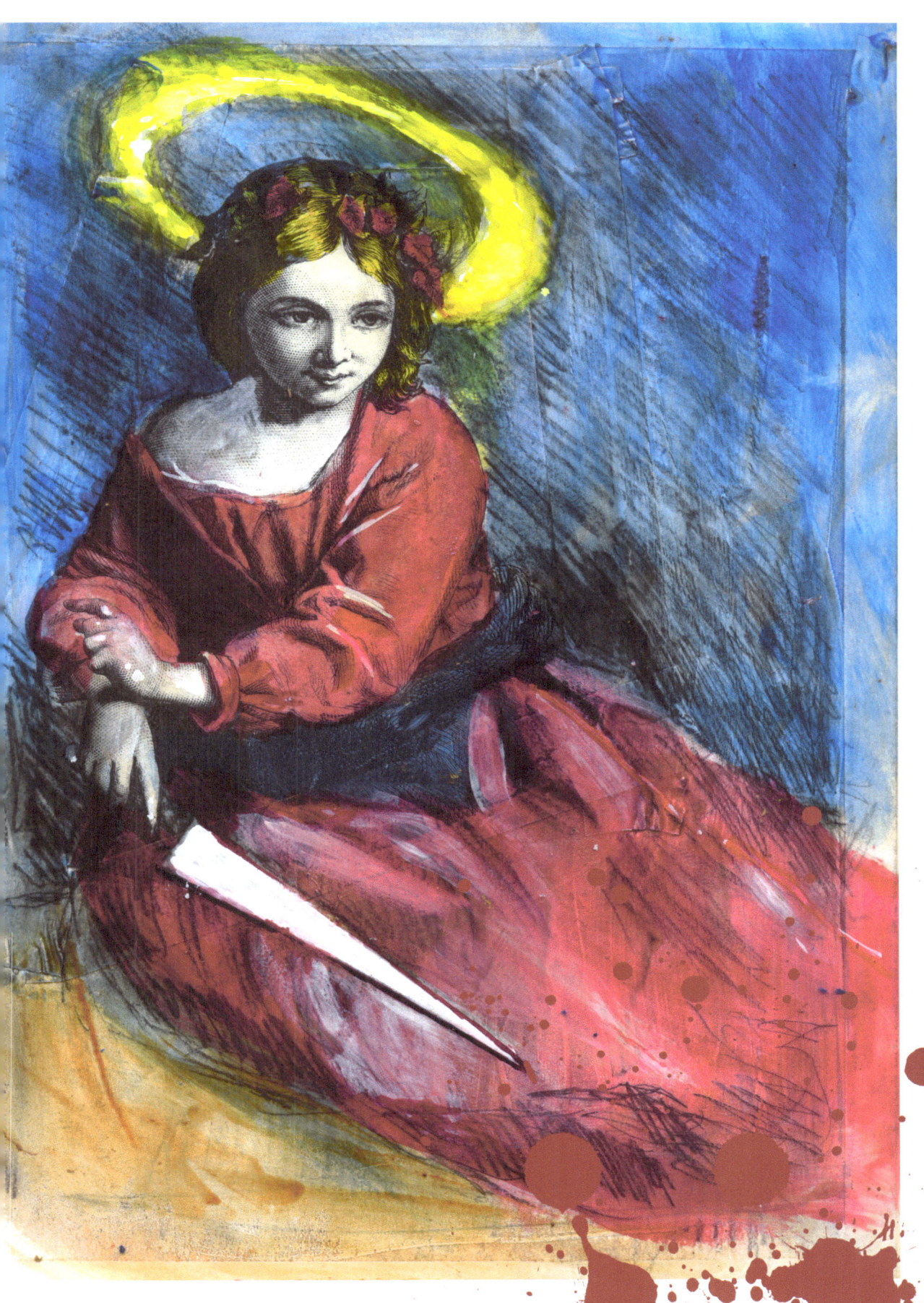

The spider fisher

Dear Sister Nancy
What's the story today?
Did you swallow the sea
Did your house run away?

Dear Sister Nancy
What did you weave?
Another tall tale
We could never believe?

Dear Sister Nancy
Did you dine with the Devil?
Did you fall down the well
Are you still bleeding pebbles?

Dear Sister Nancy
Is your creek still on fire?
Are you stark-raving mad
Or a fantastic liar?

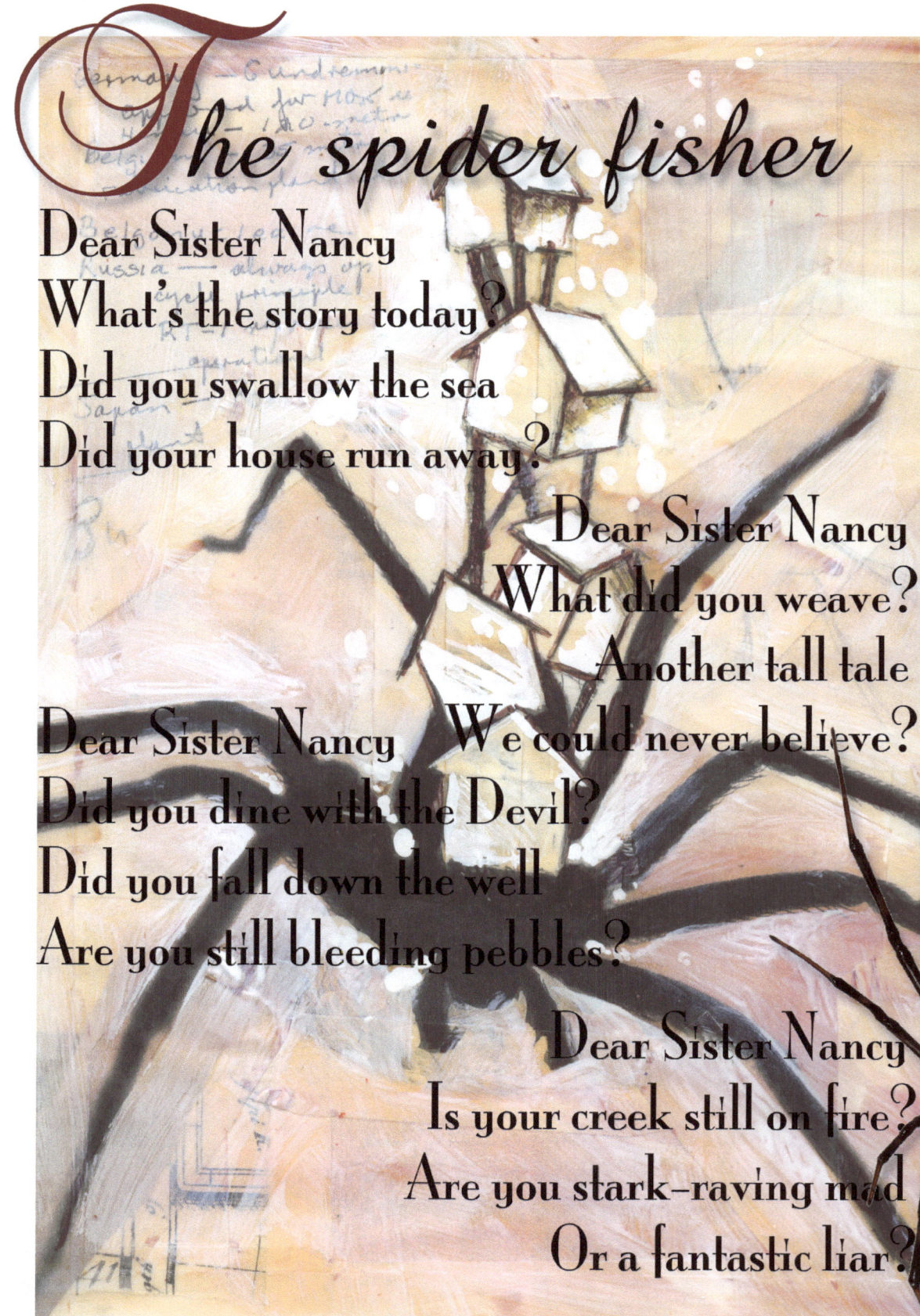

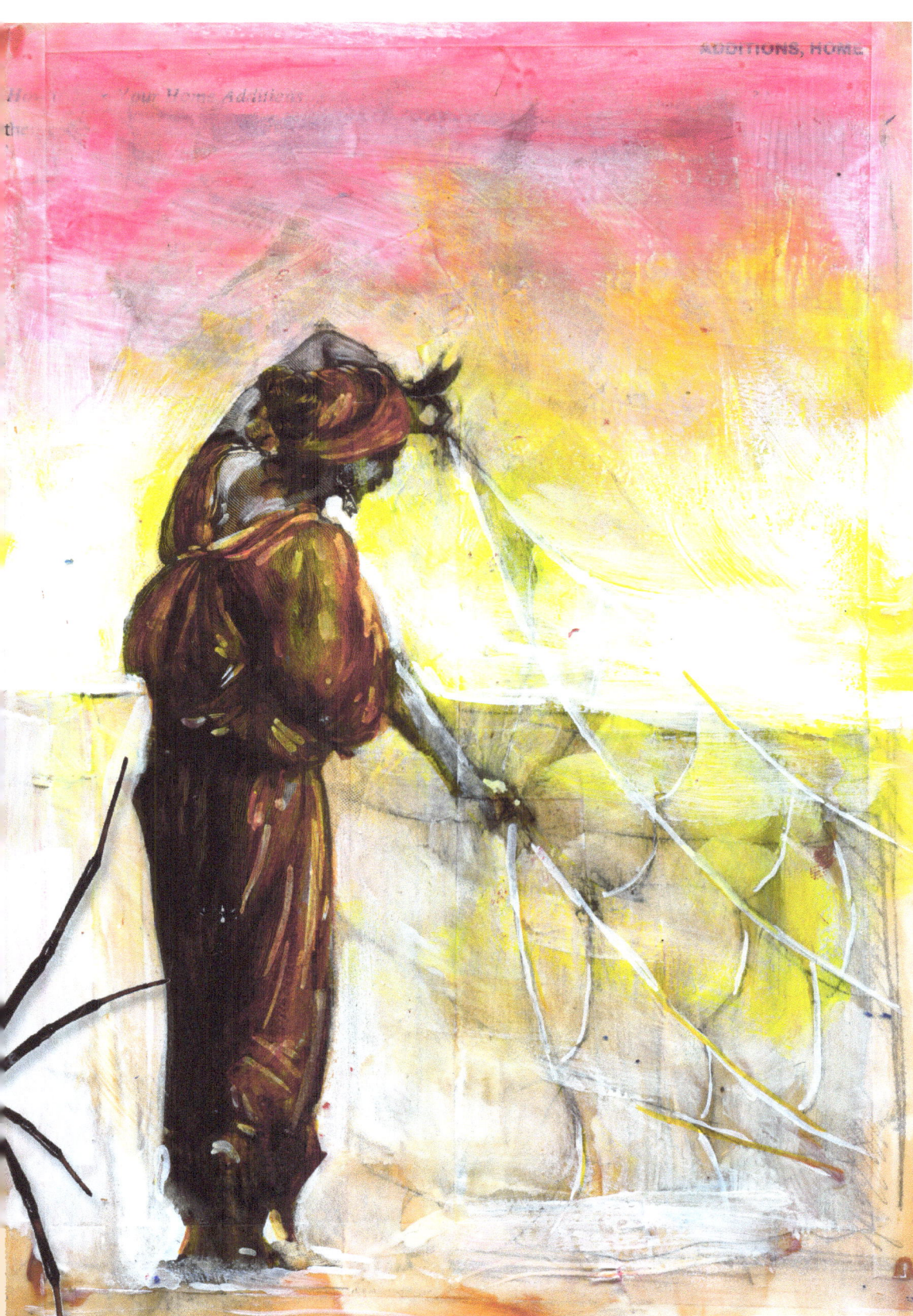

Serpentine

Ladies, please,
we must take care
To shield our suitors
from our flaws

But occasionally
it never hurts
To let them glimpse
your teeth and claws.

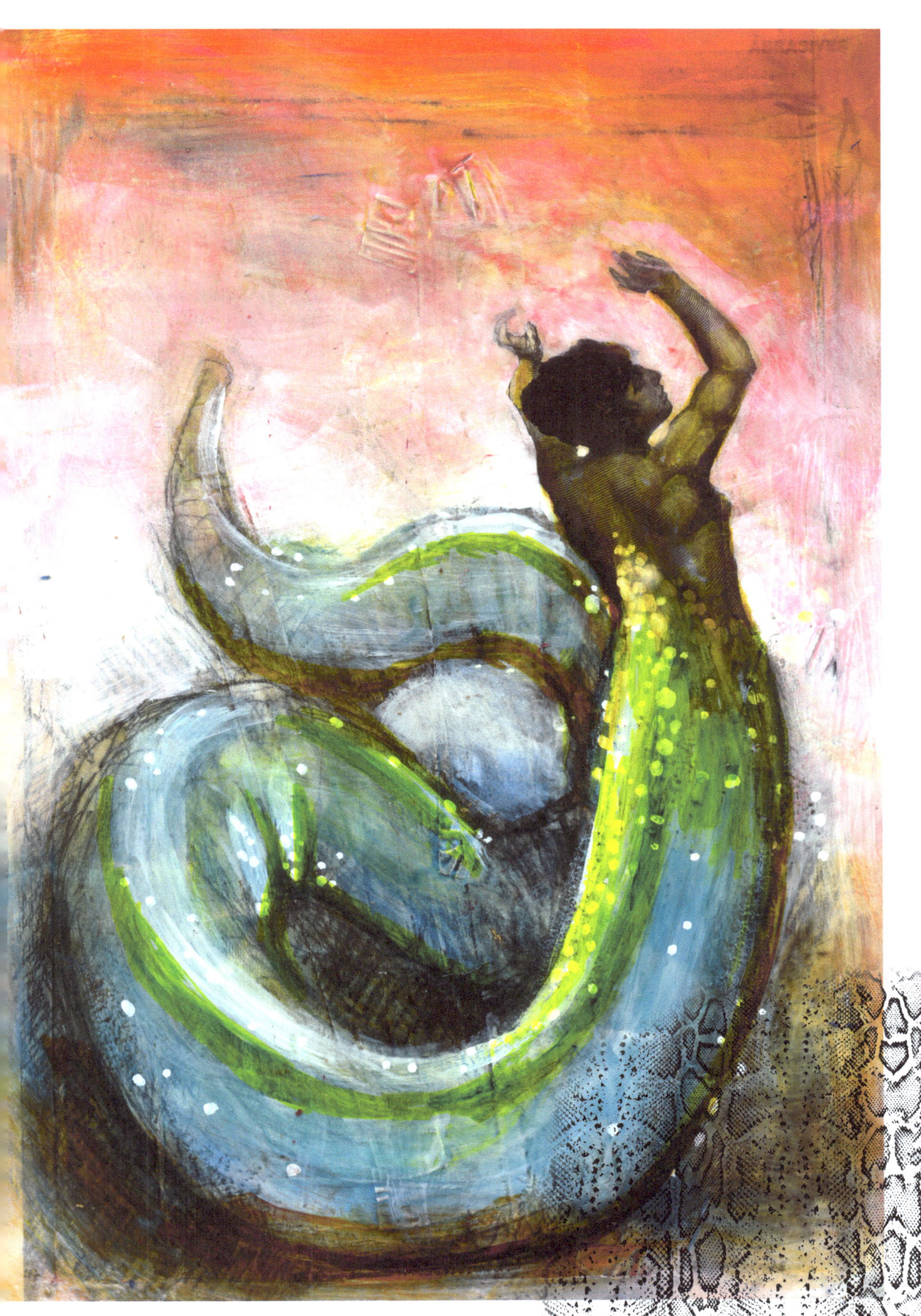

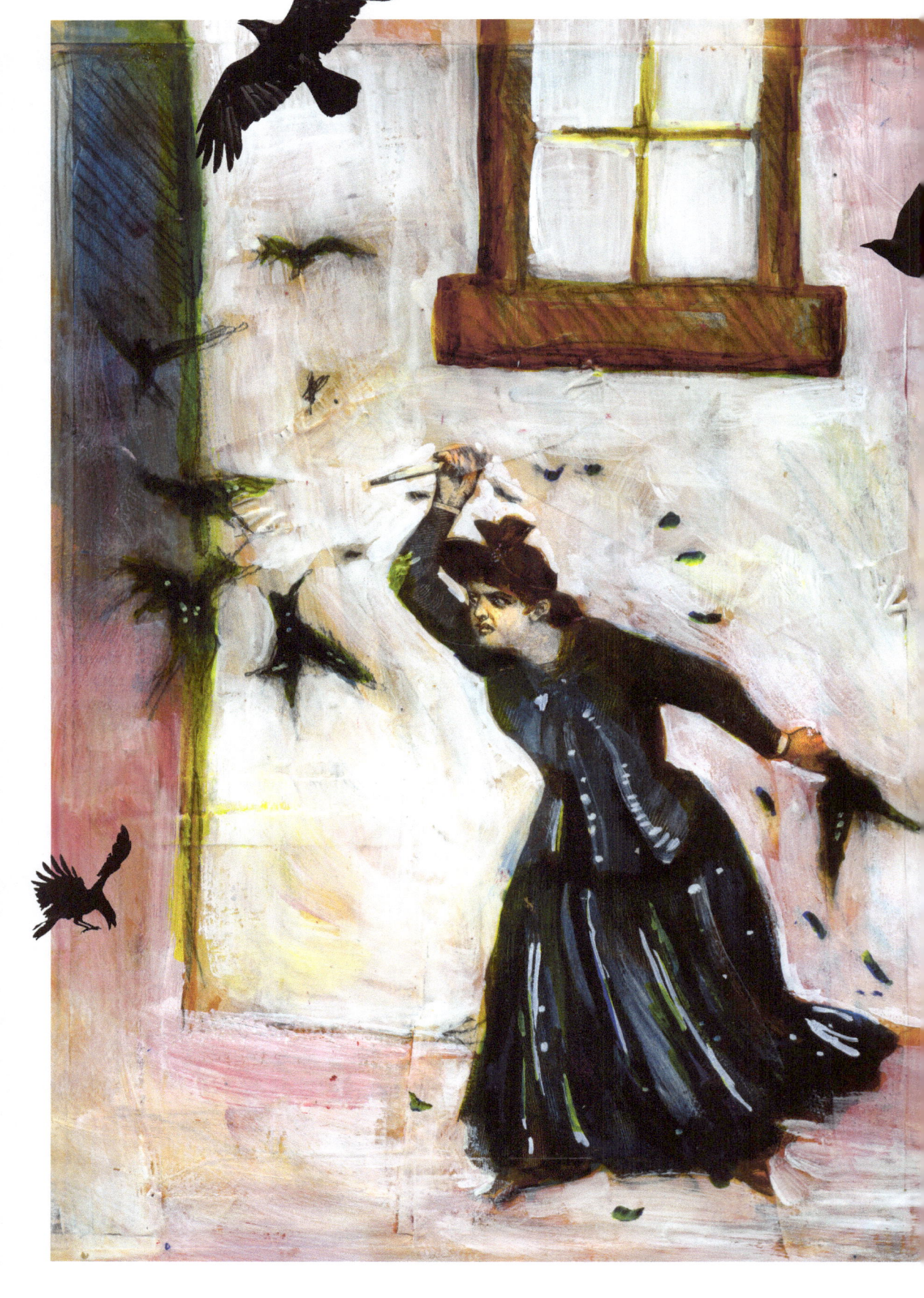

The hunter

She set all the traps

And poisoned the seed

She tethered the nets

And cut down the trees

But the sparrows arrive

Without pause or delay

They come for her soul

At the end of each day

But she will not go gently

She will not give in

She wants life eternal

She won't let them win

She's yet to surrender

She's yet to succumb

But no matter her method

The sparrows still come

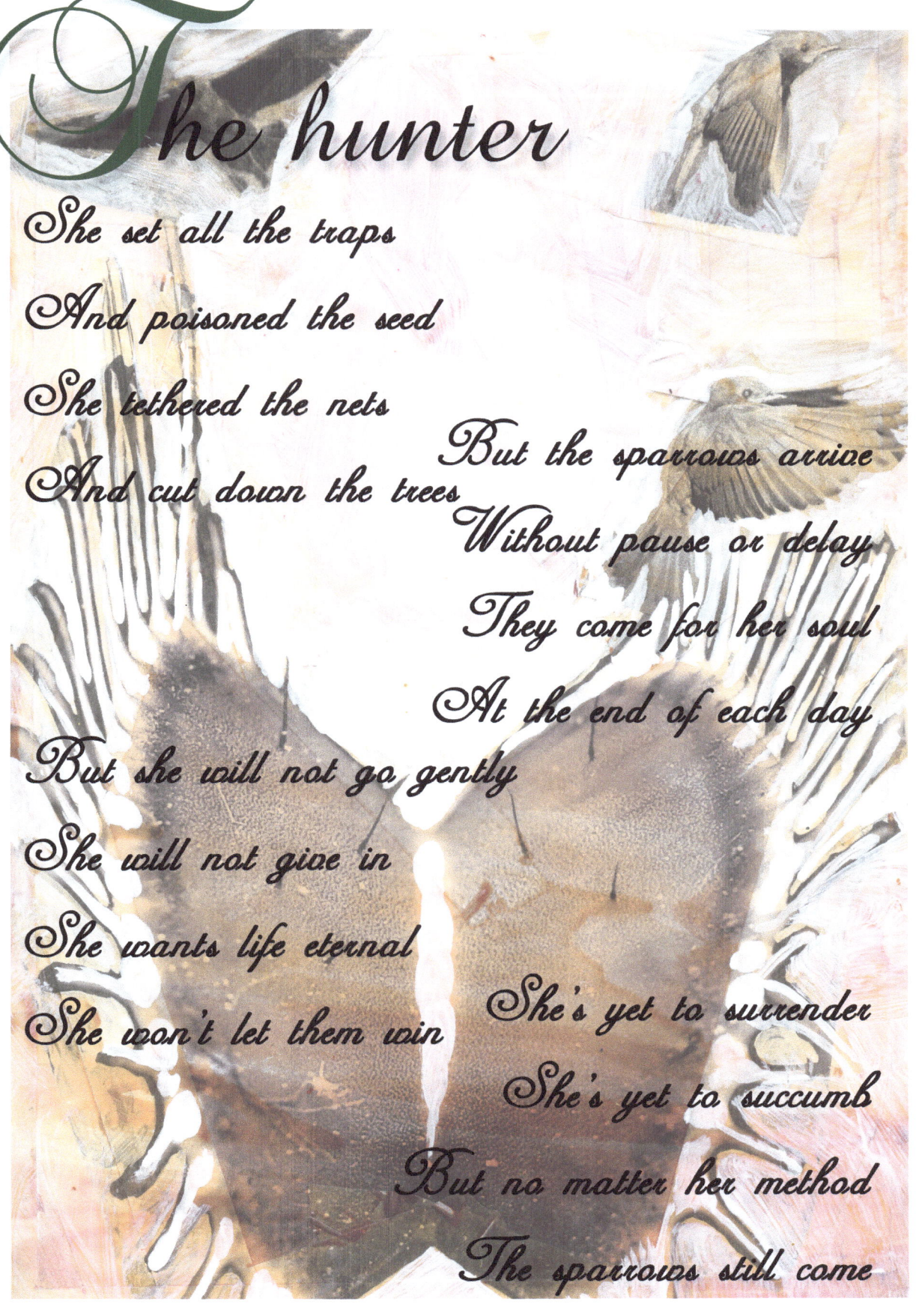

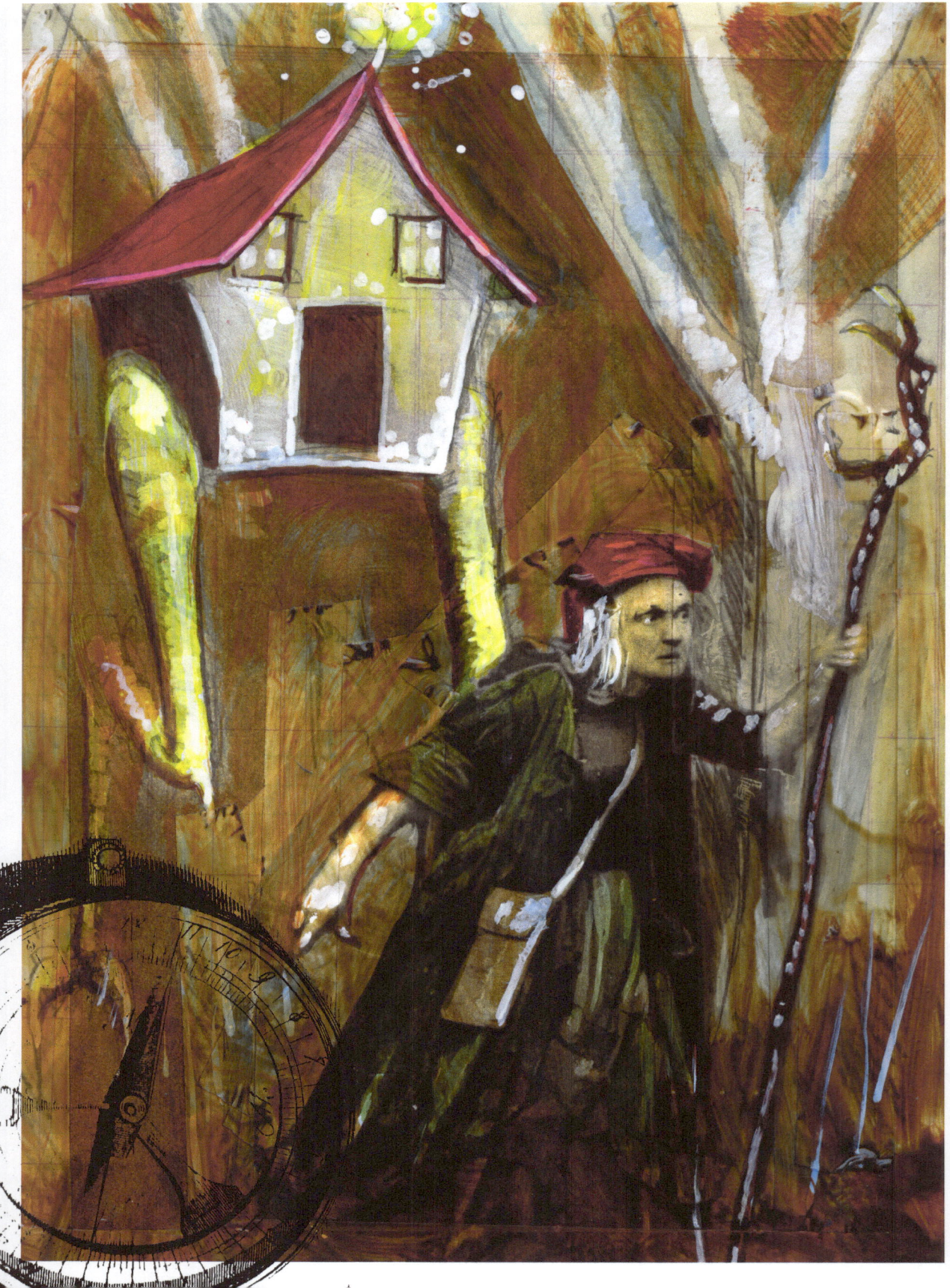

My Grandmother, the hunter

Could it be any colder
out here in the wood?
Oh, Grandmother, what shall we do?

We'll chop up the birch
And slaughter a deer
Dear child, we will make it through

Could it be any darker
out here in the wood?
Oh, Grandmother, how will we see?

We'll light up our torches
And walk by the moon
Dear child, just follow my lead

Could they be any crueler,
these ravenous wolves?
Oh, Gran,
here they come for my bones!

There's no need to cry
I'll skin them alive
Dear child, you're never alone

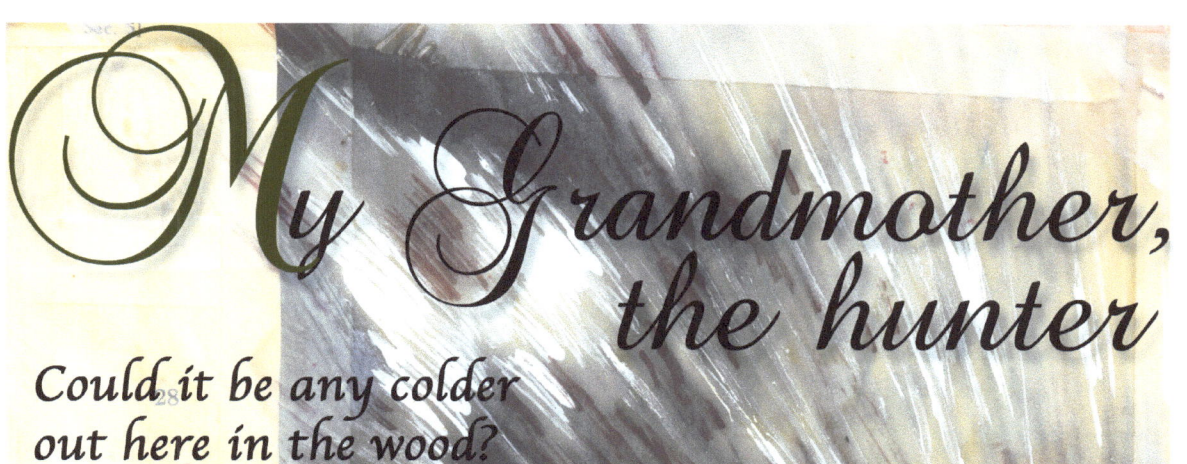

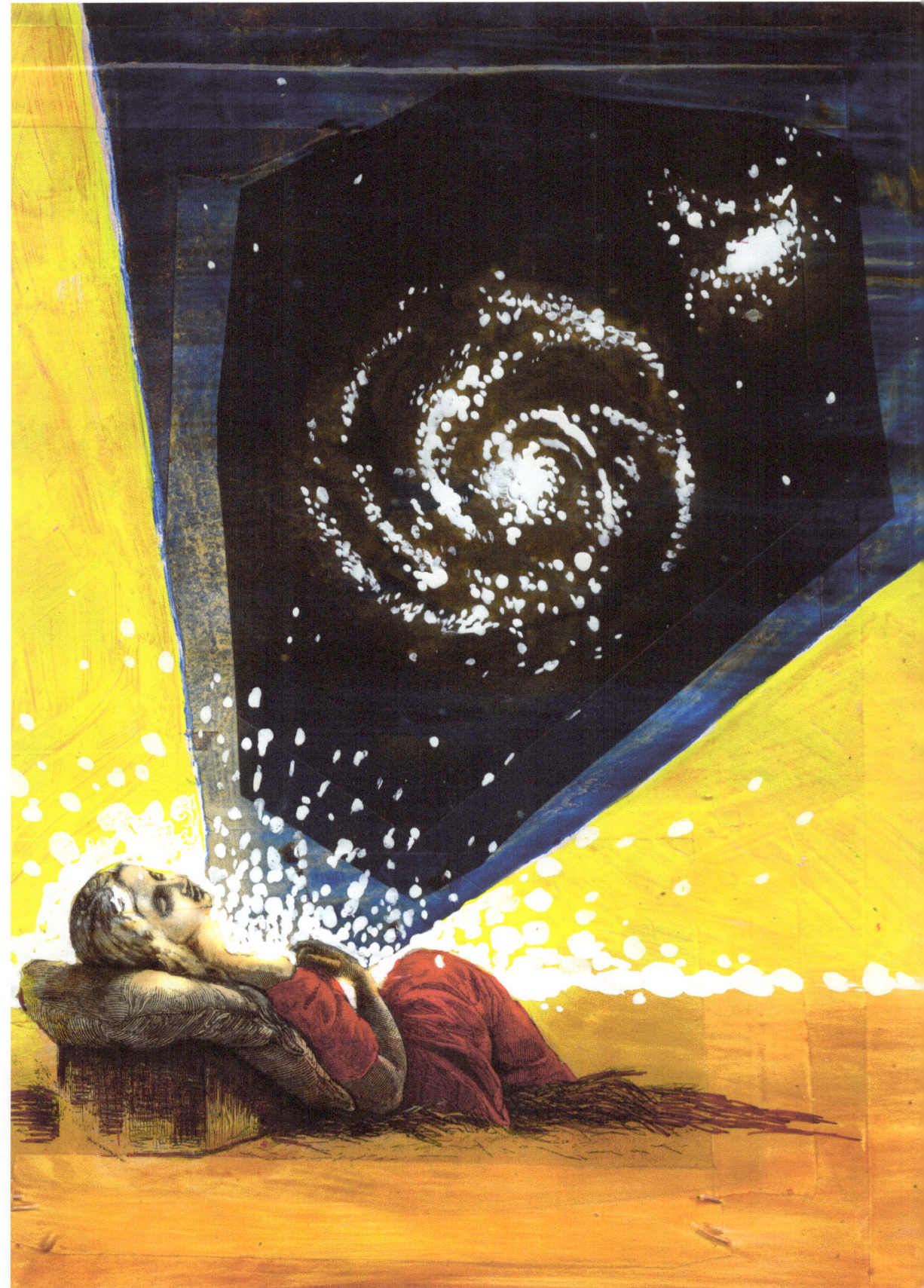

All the stary night

You take them for granted
My celestial bodies
As though they were
put there for you

        But they are not so fragile
        They hold little magic
        I know, because
        I'm the cocoon

I am Supernova
I am the Collapse
Inside I am all Galaxies
And I open myself
So that heaven appears
And that you may
create mysteries

        Let children make wishes
        Let lovers write odes
        Let madmen see beasts
        and hunters and bows
        I'll give you
        the light you desire, in turn
        If you'll try to imagine
        just how much it burns

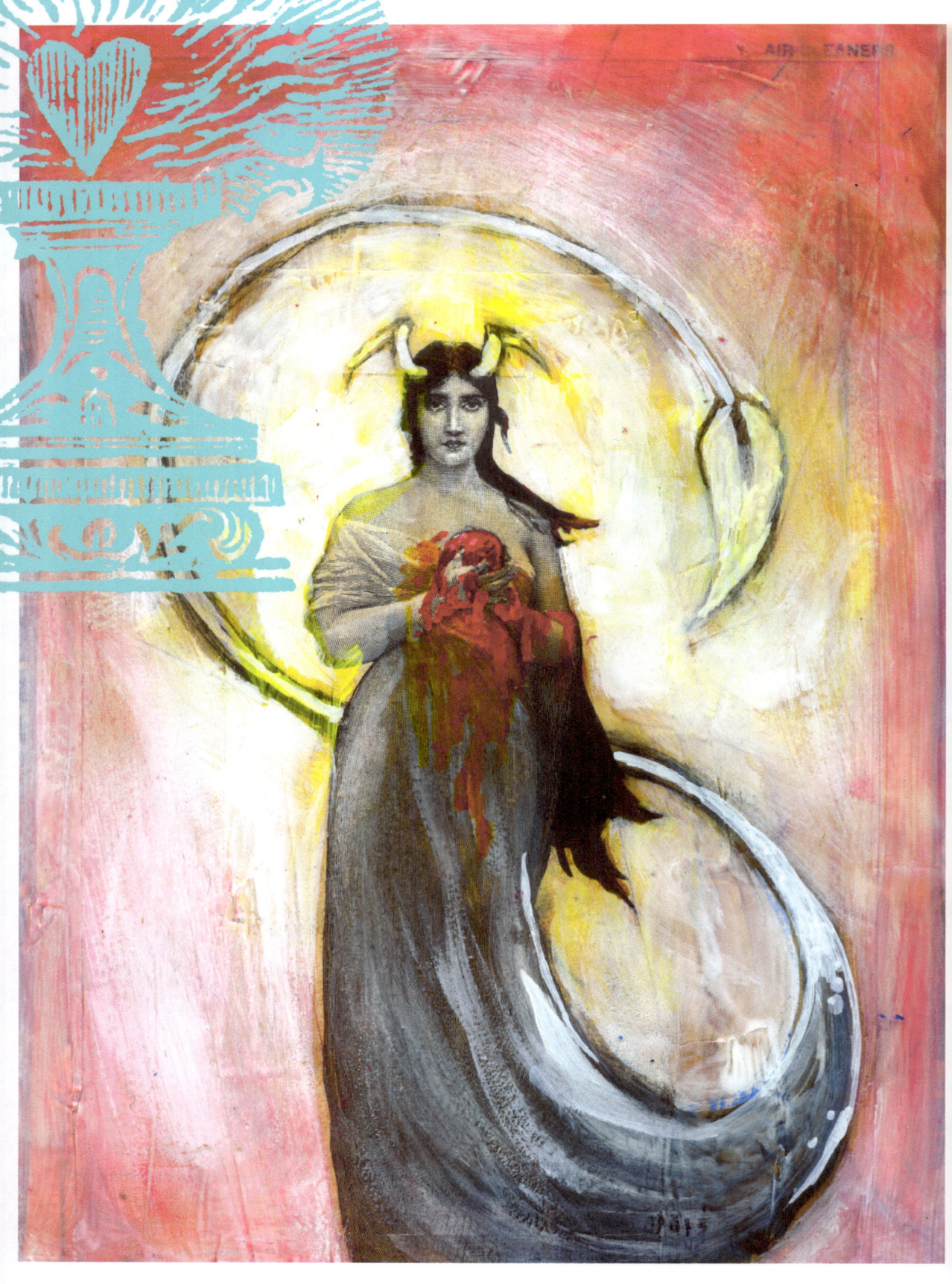

Heartless

You feel too much
He used to say
So quick to give your heart away
You must let go
Of such ideals
Of fairy tales
And golden fields
The world is cold
You can't survive
With starlight burning in your eyes
And so I heard
And understood
And clawed in deeply as I could
I dug away at flesh and bone
I tore my heart out of her home
I buried her
Deep in the ground
And left no marker to be found
I carried on with calloused skin
And never felt a thing again
And now I've come this far alone
He wonders why I've grown so cold

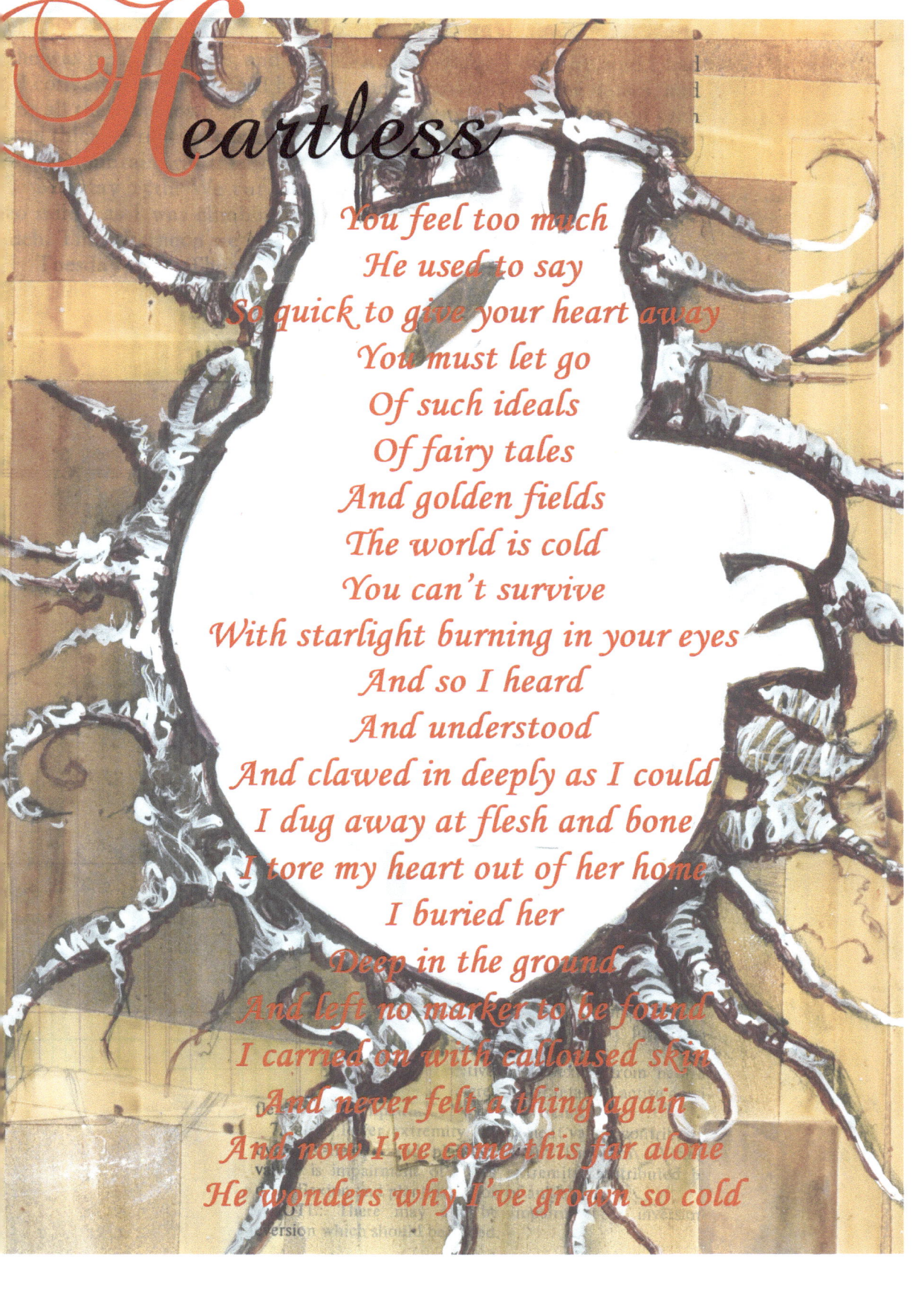

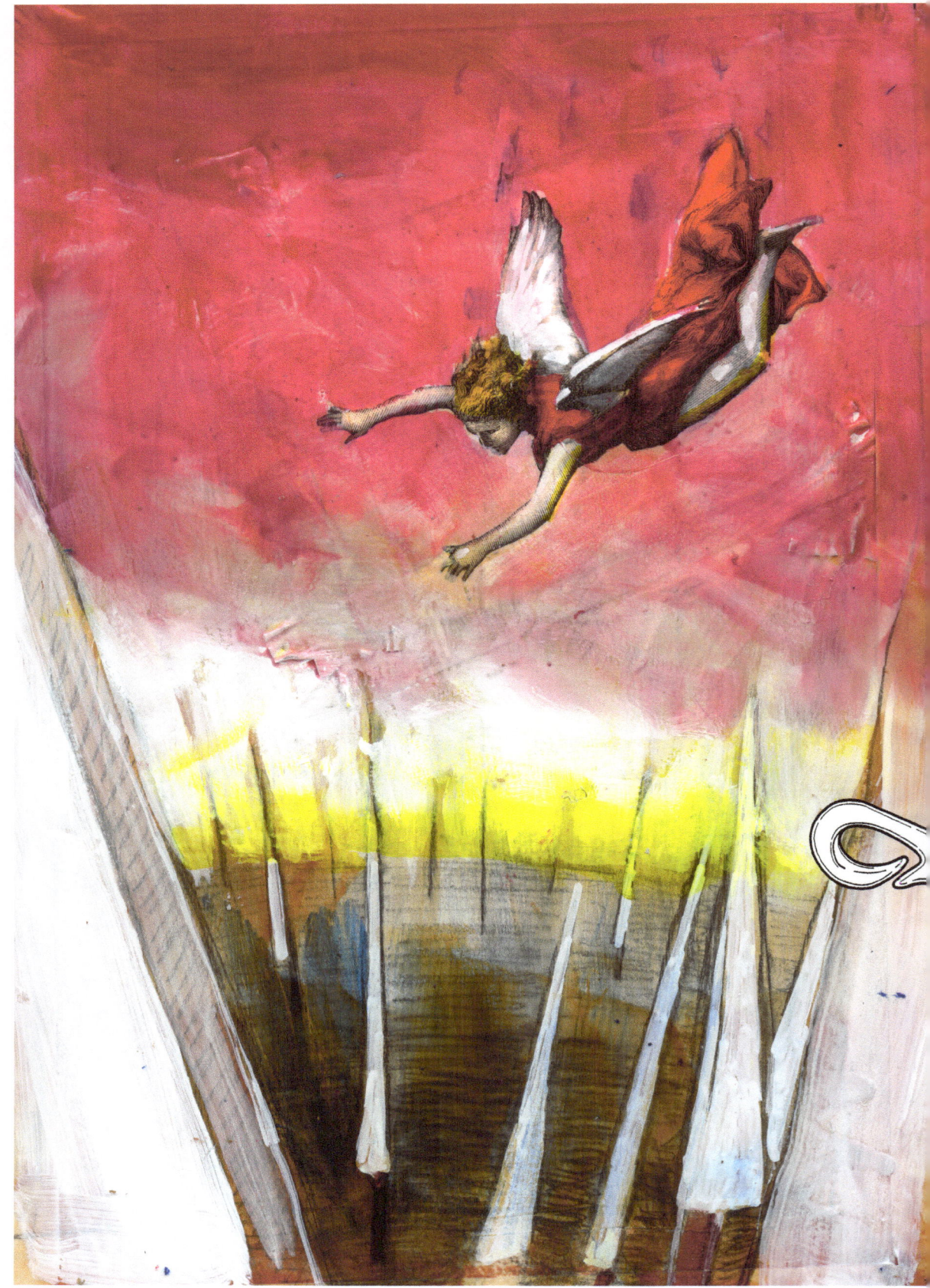

Descent

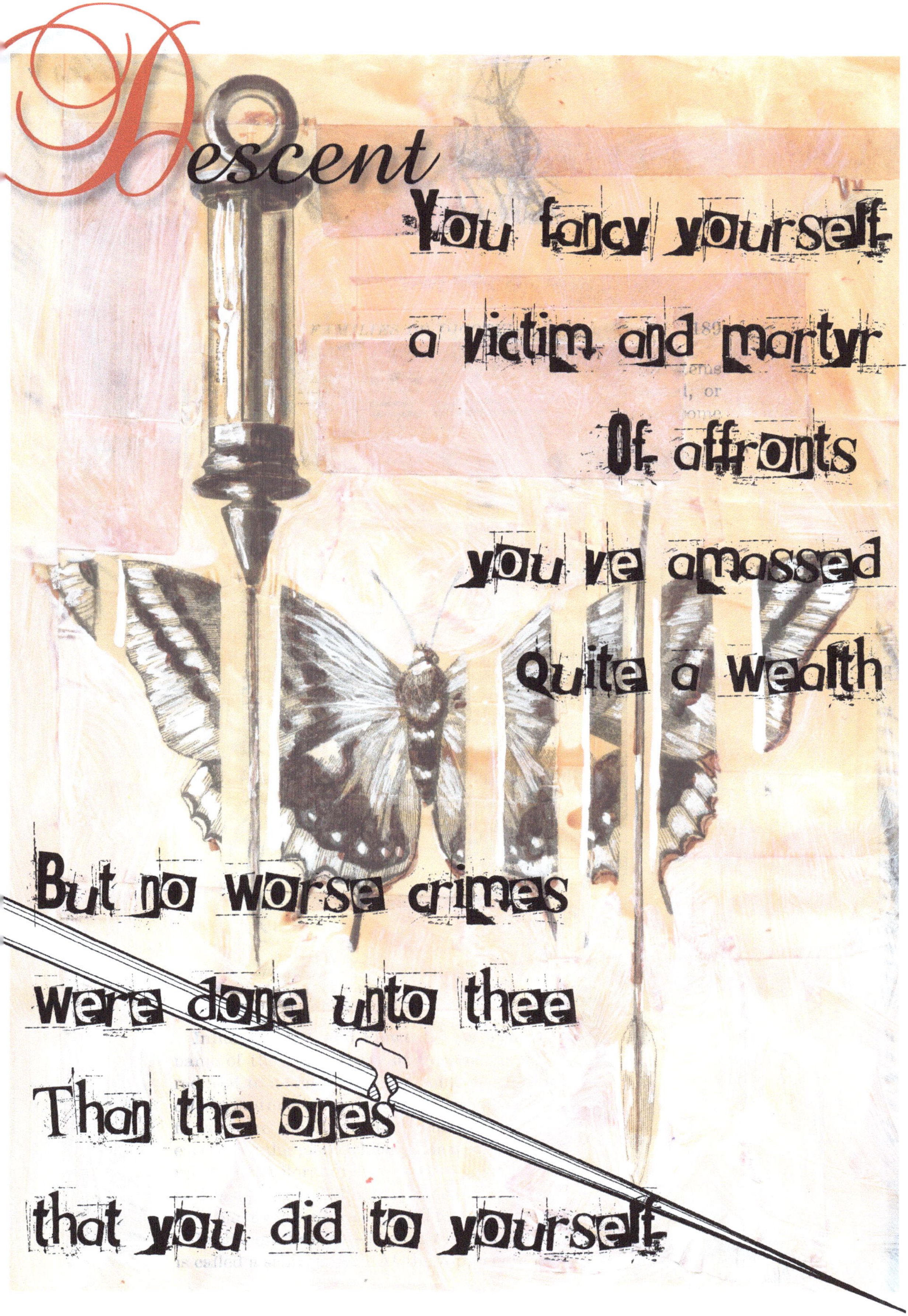

You fancy yourself
a victim and martyr
Of affronts
you've amassed
Quite a wealth

But no worse crimes
were done unto thee
Than the ones
that you did to yourself

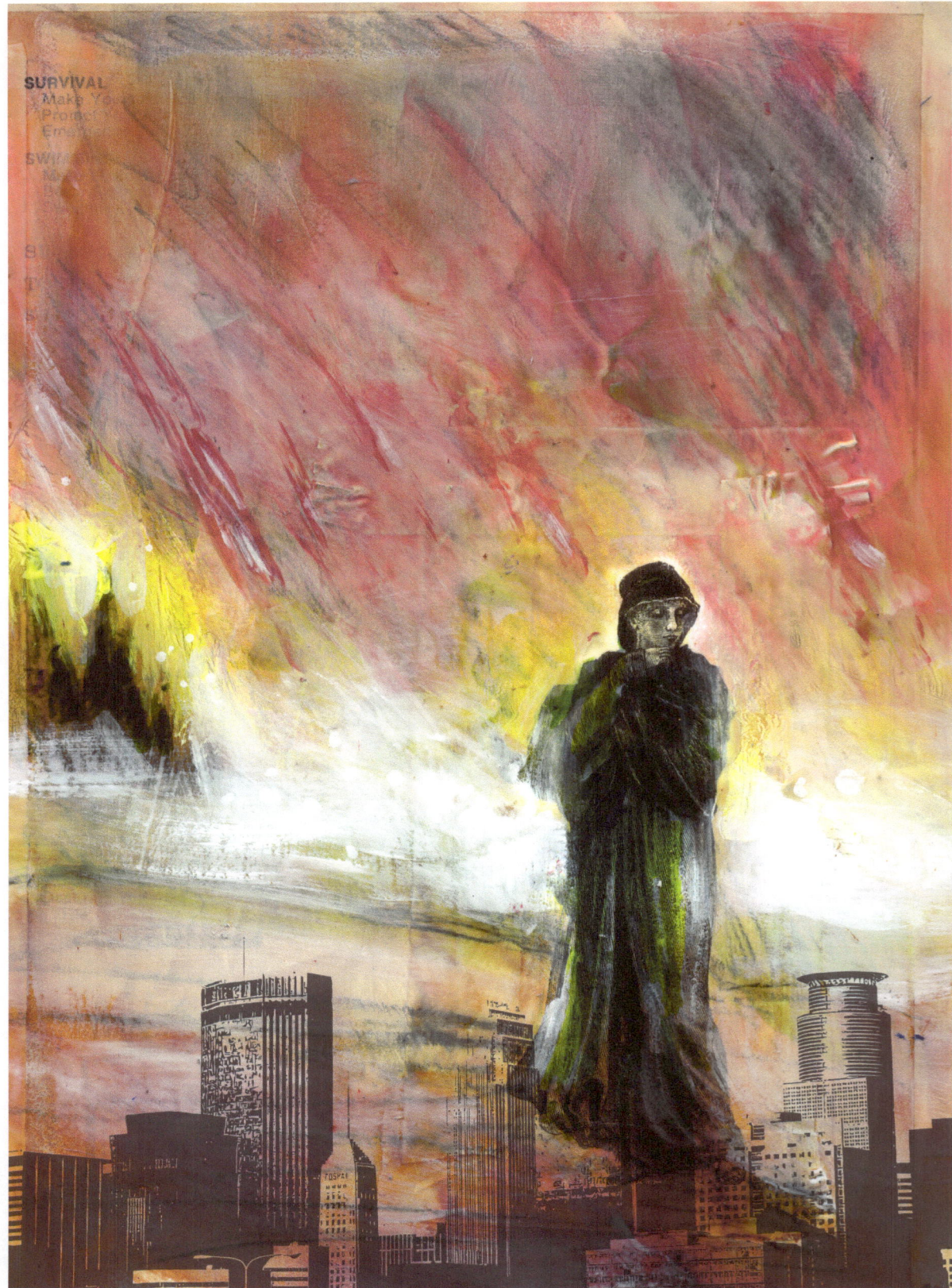

The burner

You see that woman on the road?
They call her Immolaine
She doesn't wish to be alone
And clearly she's in pain
                For something in her burns so deep
                    That everywhere she roams
                    A fire lights, consuming all
                      Or so the story goes

And children taunt with vicious games
Immolaine, O, Immolaine
Now you're going up in flames!'
She dreads to hear them speak her name
And so she never stops for long
                  She wanders day and night
                  She tires of the burning stench
                      As her soul ignites

And mothers tell their wayward young
To watch for Immolaine
And if they see her on the road
They'd better pray for rain

Seduction machine

What demon is this
Descended upon me
Riding my back till I'm broken
Controlling my hands
And my mouth
And my hips
Formalities all left unspoken

I never agreed
She never concedes
I'm left on my knees
When she's through
But I know she is near
She's drawn to my fear
Wearing it like a perfume

I no longer dread
That she'll leave me for dead
And she knows
That I no longer fight it
But the thing I fear most
From this red carnal ghost
Is that I'm beginning to like it

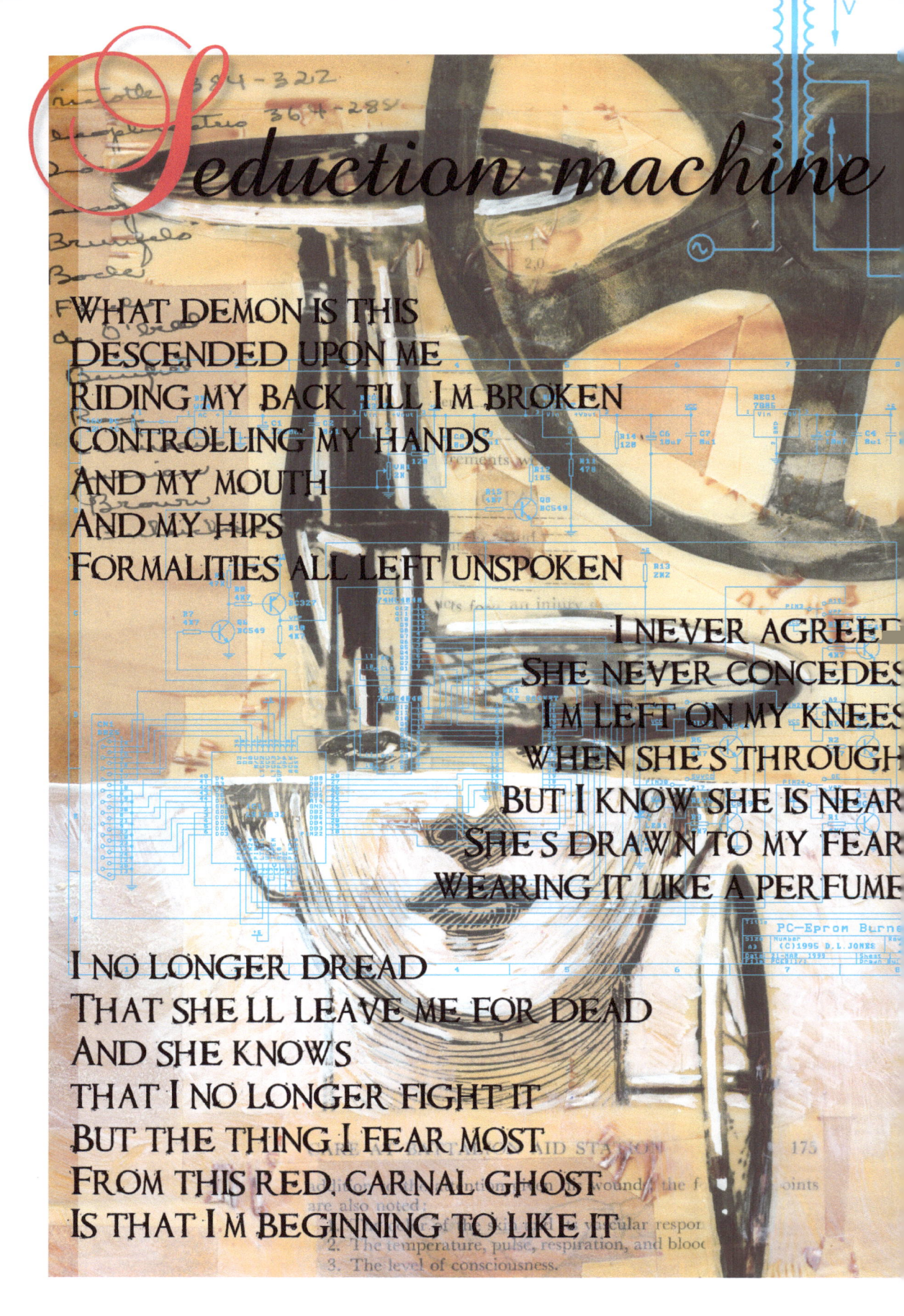

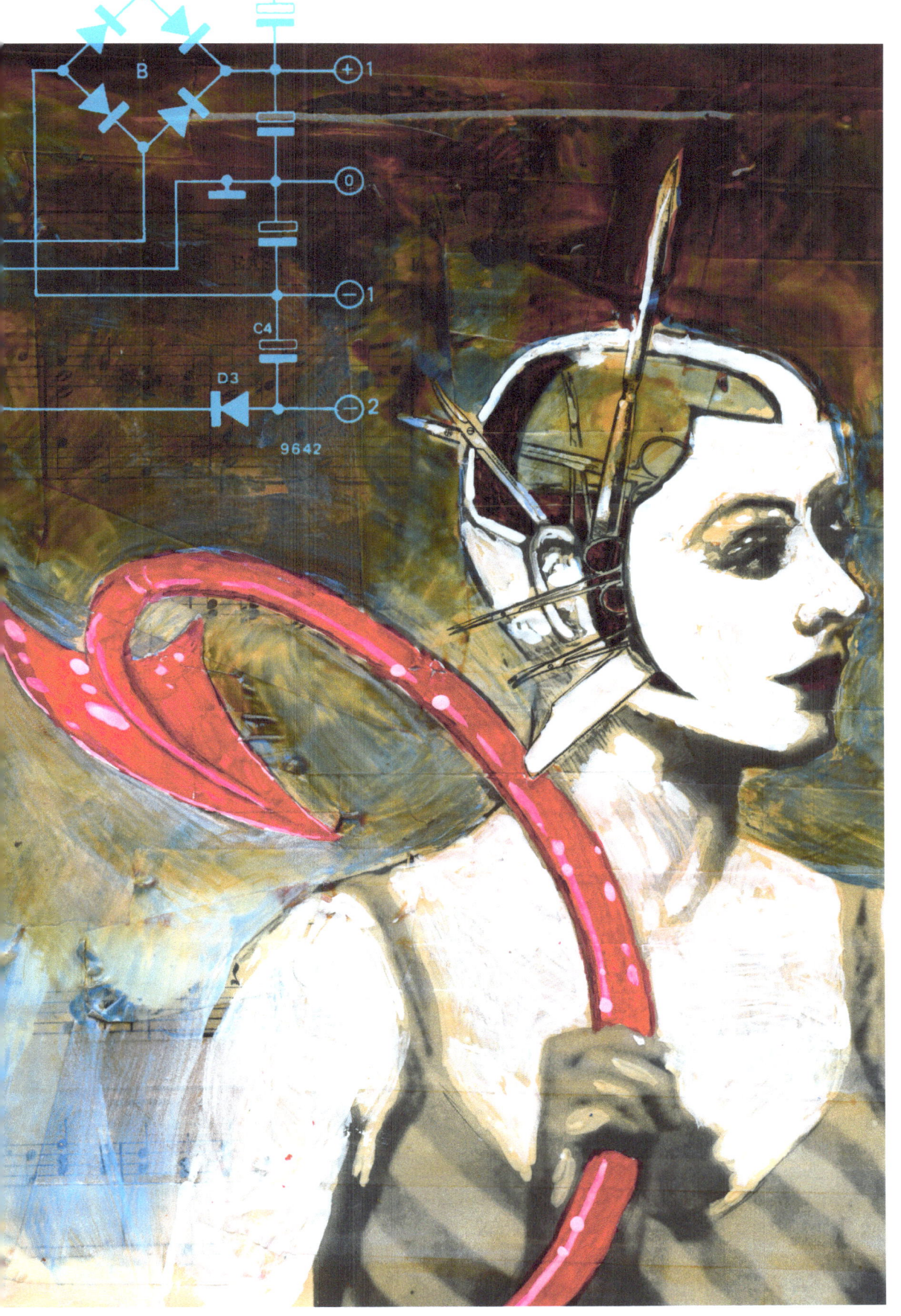

The queen of the 9th ward

My sister, my river
You always were crazy
Some days you are wild
Some days you are lazy

My lover, my city
You always were strong
You may get knocked down
But never for long

My brothers, my spirits
They help ease the pain
They're there when I'm cryin'
They help keep me sane

My Papa, the warden
He watches the gate
I call out his name
And alter my fate

My mother, my vengeance
My heart and my dove
She taught me to fight
And she taught me to love

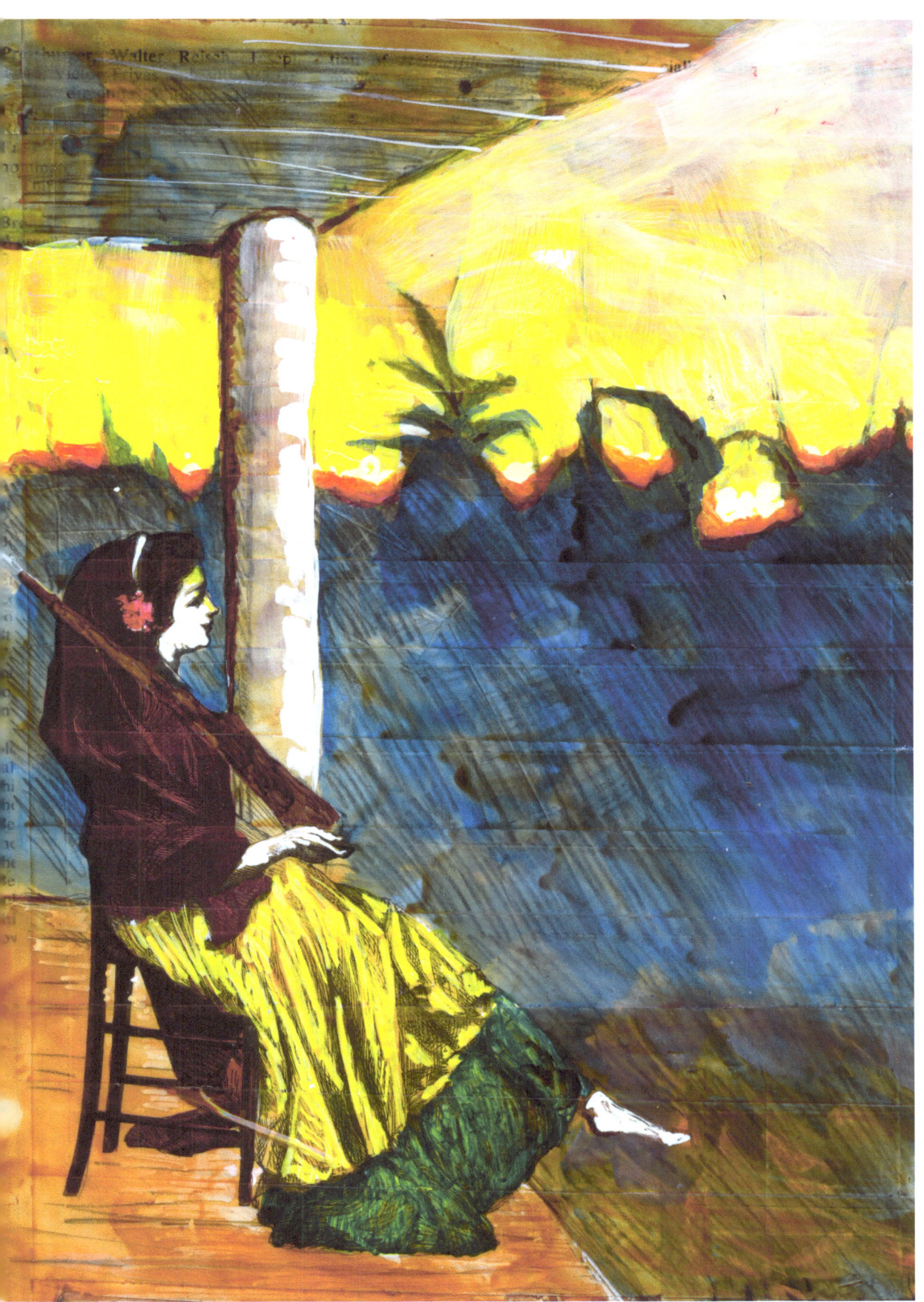

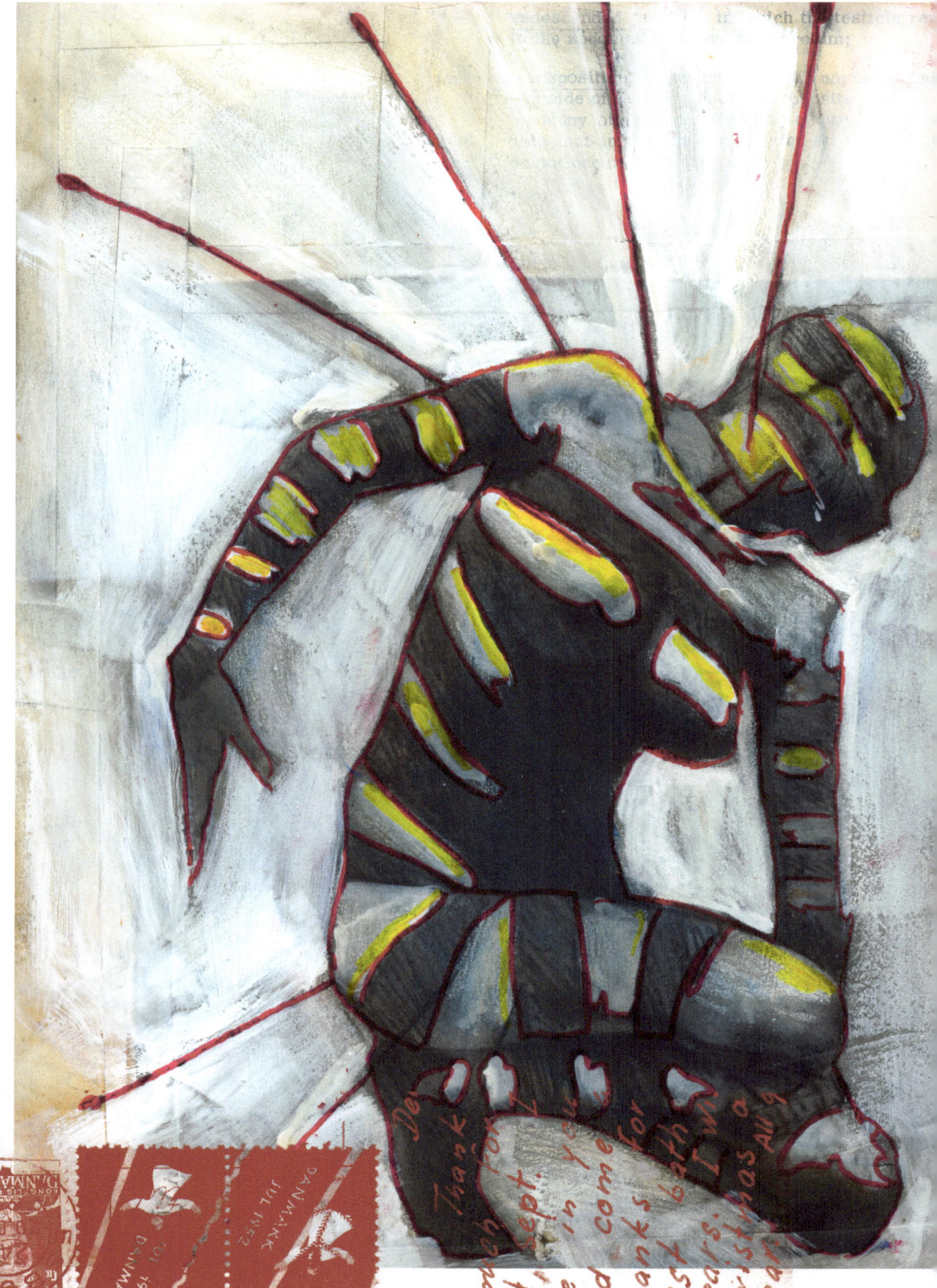

Behold the hive queen

When she asked you to build
You did not hesitate
What wouldn't you do for her beauty?

When she asked you to fight
For the colony's sake
You answered her call of duty

You're happy to serve
Give her all she deserves
Your loyalty - she'd never abuse it

When she asks you to strike
Though you'll be torn apart
I'm just wondering if you will do it

Mary abattoir

Are we made of our words?
Or our thoughts and our deeds
Or of light bound by flesh?
Or our hopes and our dreams

Are we angels or devils?
Or souls trapped in bone?
All things poetic
All things unknown

While our spirits may soar
And our hearts, they will beat
When the flame is extinguished
All that's left is the meat

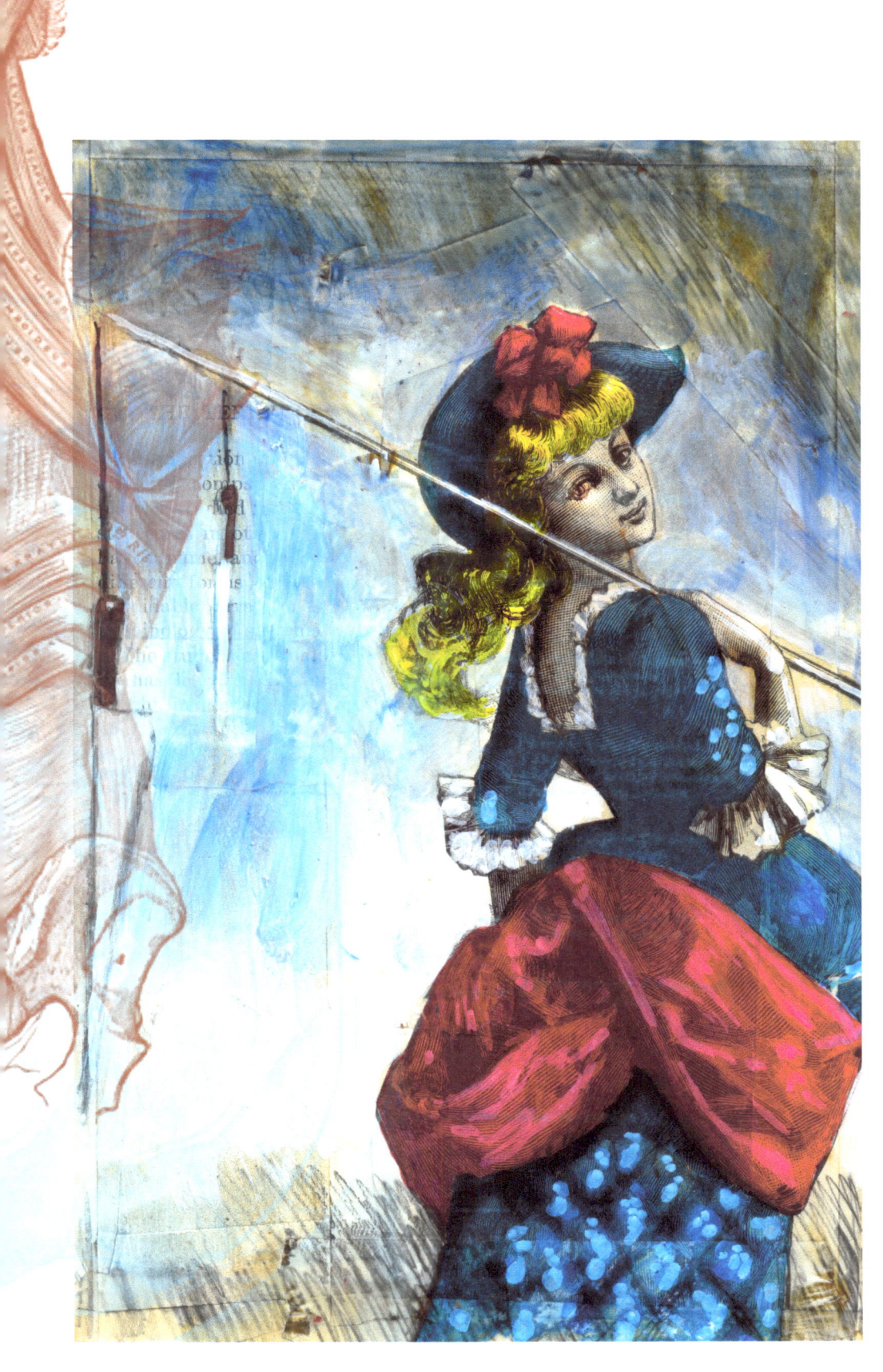

Mother of water

She's here every night
At the end of the bar
Watching the world stumble by
They say she was something,
a long time ago
You can tell
by the look in her eye

But that was before
When the world still believed
In Sirens and magic
And things you can't see

Yet she doesn't seem sad
That the world has moved on
She remembers the tides
She remembers her song

And now she's just fine
With her rum and her secrets
She once ruled the sea
She once was its spirit
How does she start over?
How does she begin?

I just drink it all in Doll
I just drink it all in

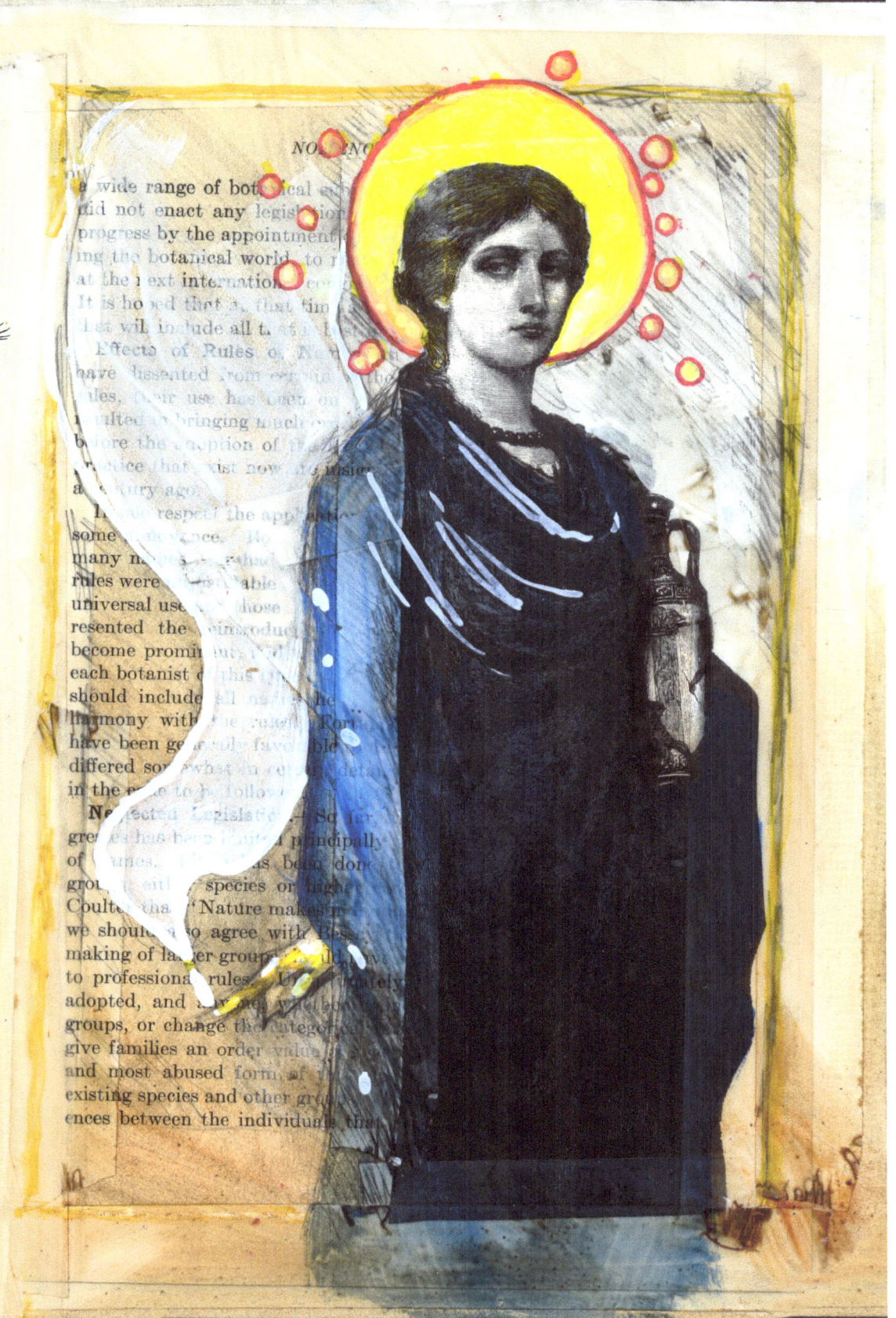

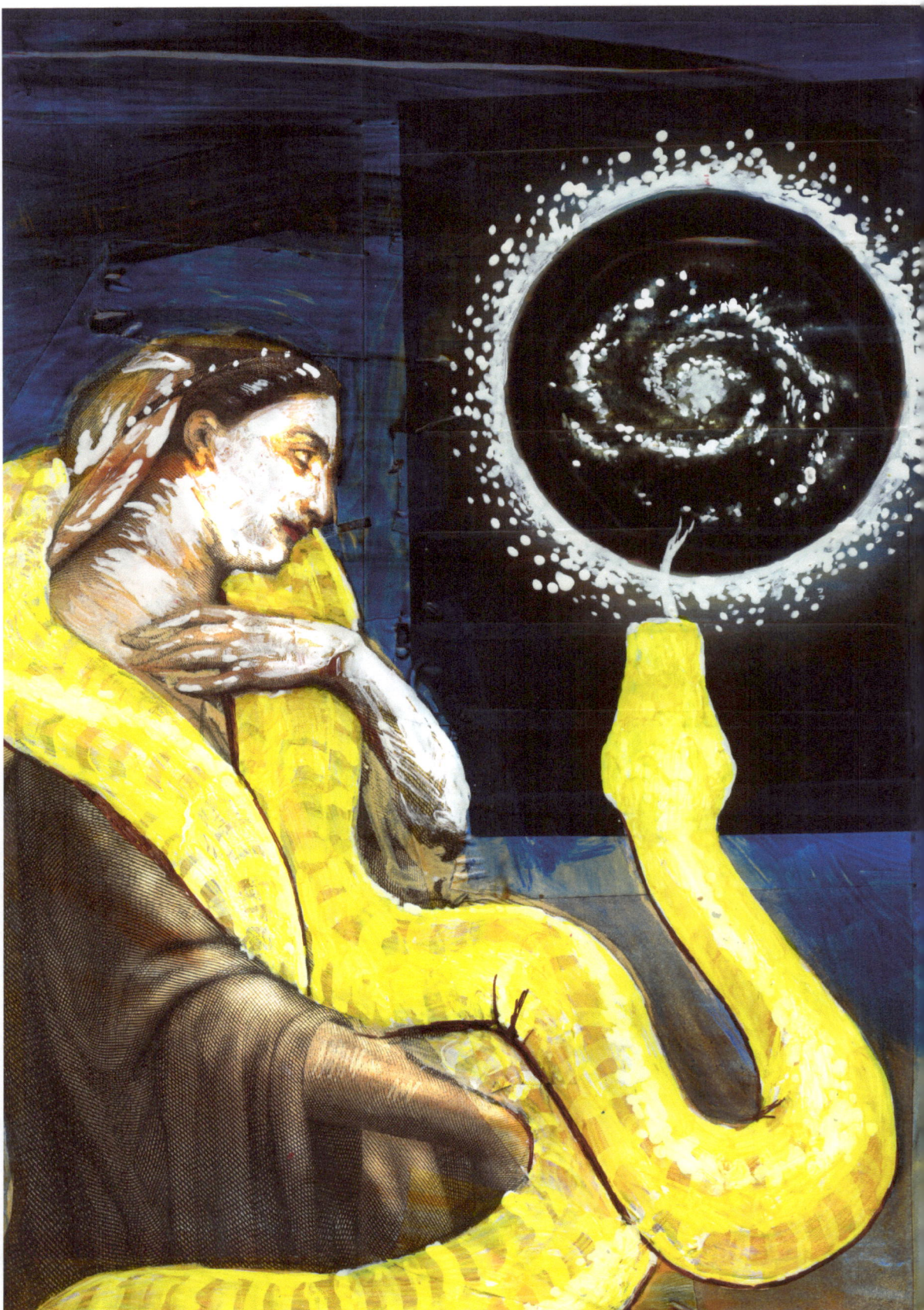

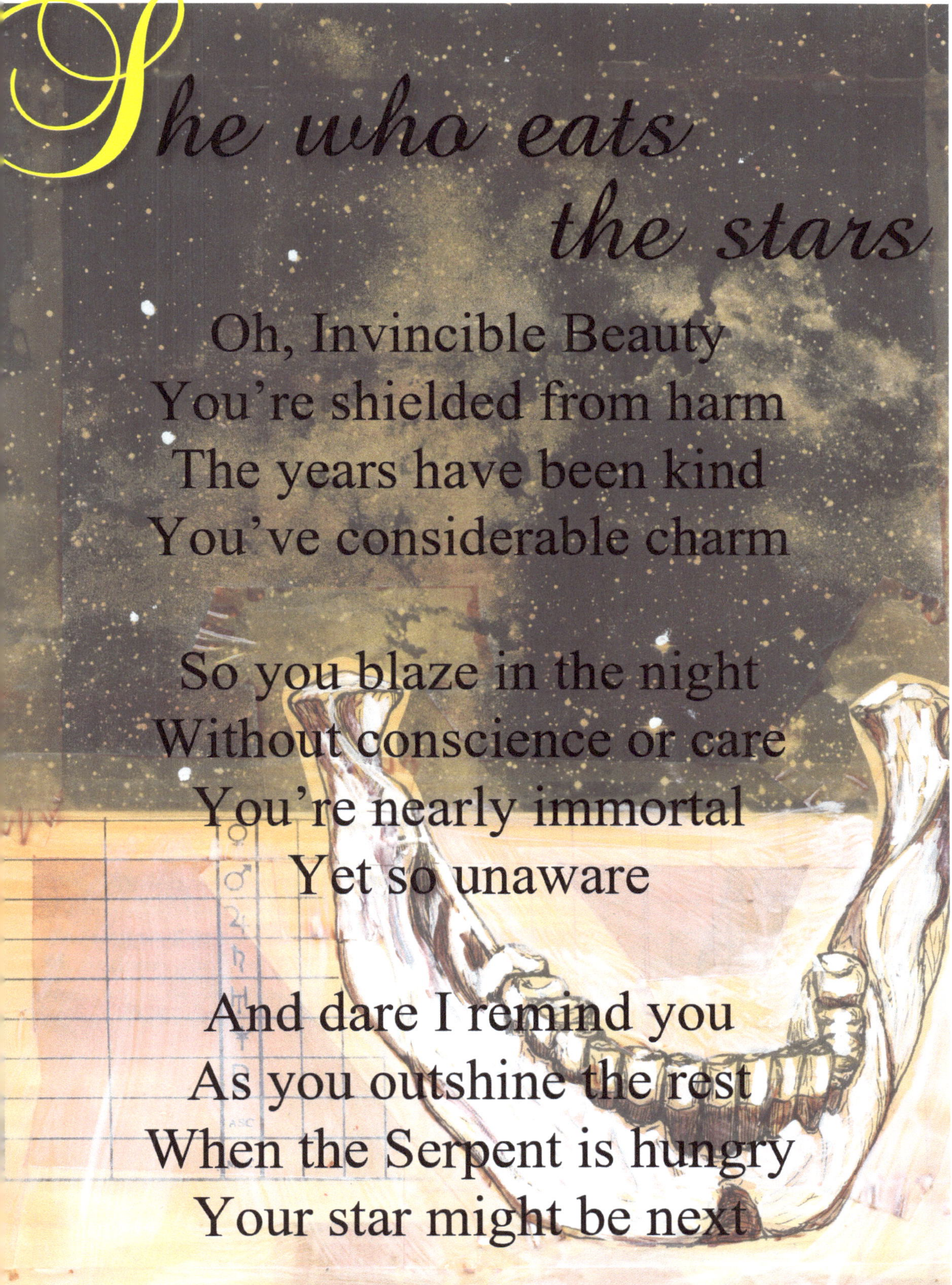

She who eats the stars

Oh, Invincible Beauty
You're shielded from harm
The years have been kind
You've considerable charm

So you blaze in the night
Without conscience or care
You're nearly immortal
Yet so unaware

And dare I remind you
As you outshine the rest
When the Serpent is hungry
Your star might be next

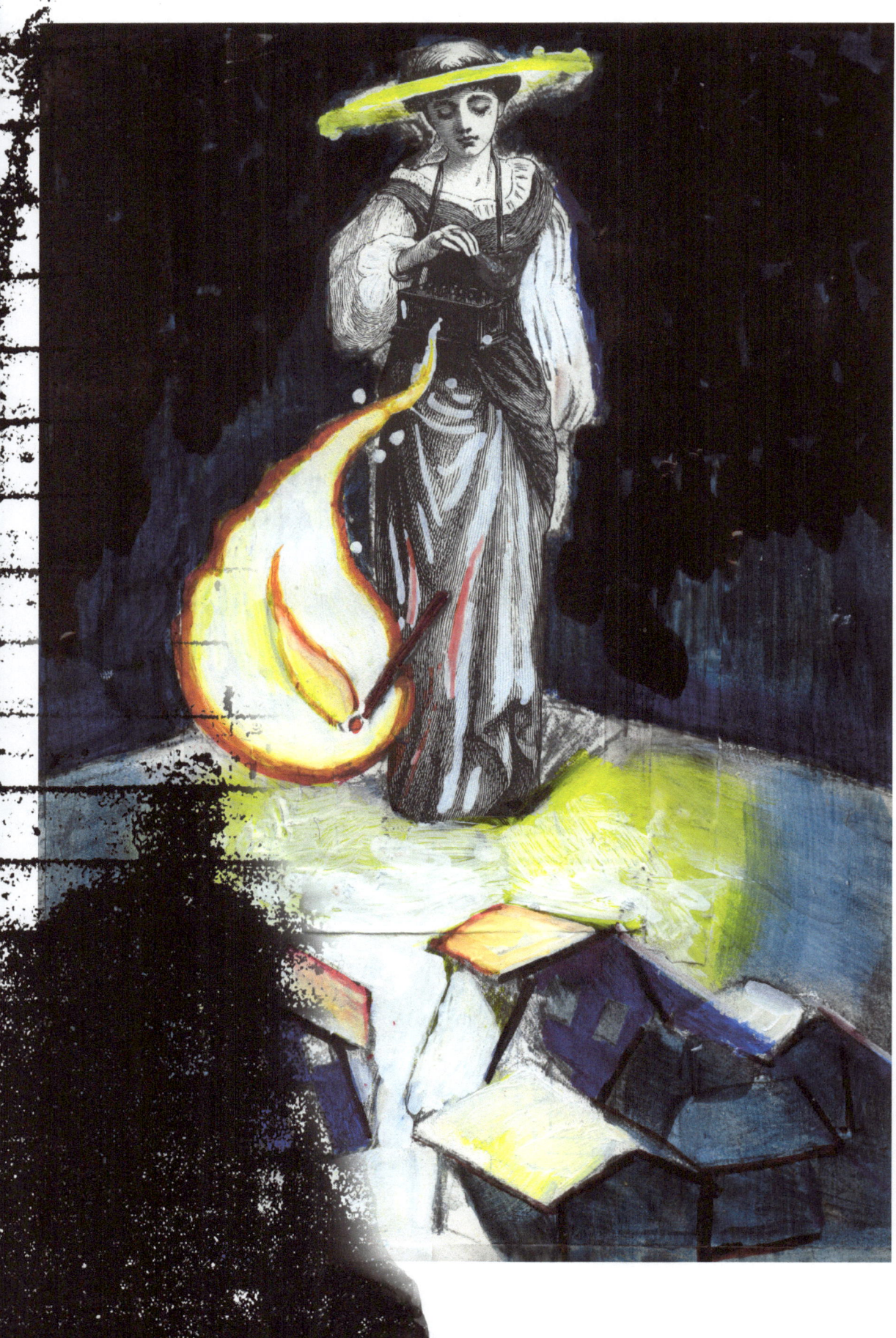

I am the end of your city

I am the Destroyer
I say with a smile
My mission is simple and clear
This city -your kingdom-
Is wretched and vile
And brimming with
violence and fear

You misused your tools
And acted like fools
Your greed
and your hubris prevailed
But the moment has come
You're revealed in the sun
And the Daughters
will see how you've failed

So I call your disease
And summon your liars
And gather your criminals 'round
I am the Destroyer
I'll cleanse you by fire
And burn your whole world
to the ground

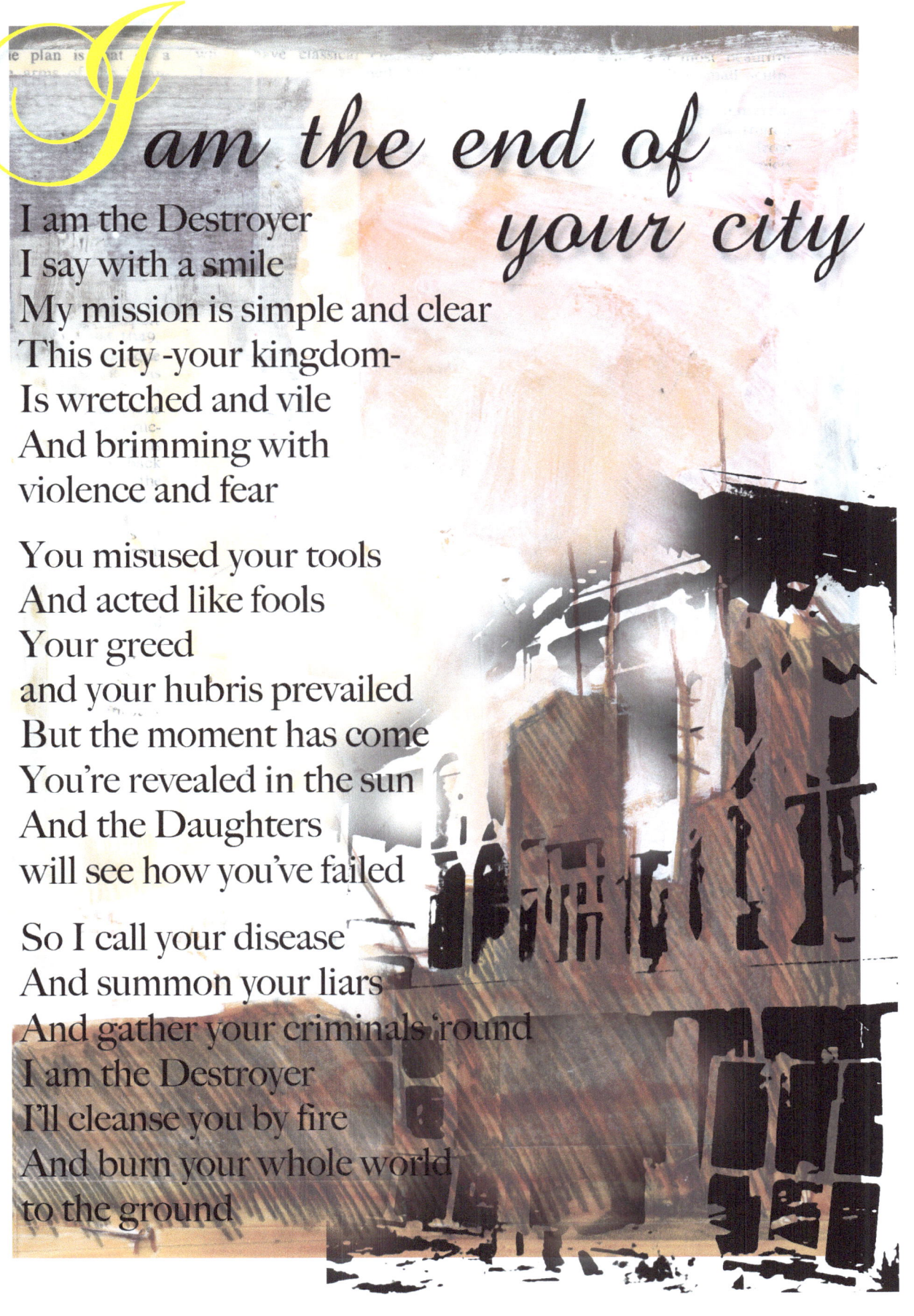

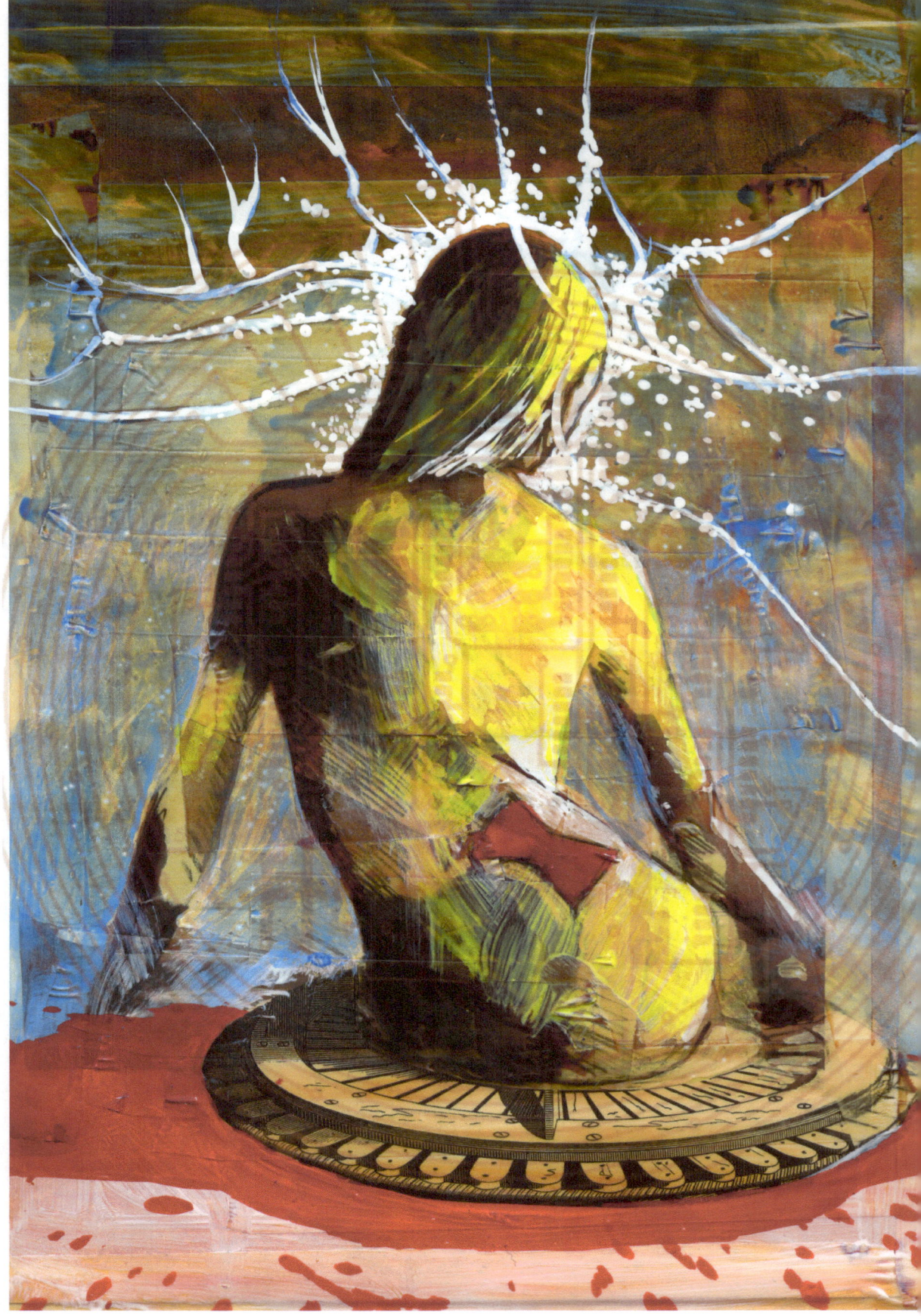

Poison machine

When she was a child
Her kisses were sweet
Like glistening sugar
Brushed on your cheek

And just like a child
She believed what he said~
That monster that slithered
His way to her bed

He dried up Swan Lake
And he burned down the Palace
He filled her with fear
And with pain and with malice

Her kisses grew toxic
Her joy turned to doubt
And the spark of her spirit
Was slowly put out

But you see in her eyes
That child, so pure
Still waiting for someone
To come with a cure

You may wish to believe
You can help her pull through
But despite your intentions
She'll poison you, too.

All that remains is me and the loss of thee

It's just the same old story
And you know how it goes
I'm tired of explaining
I'm weary of your woes

There is no god in heaven
There is no place called hell
There is no faerie kingdom
Or place where angels dwell

Your faith is placed in nothing
Your vanity is queen
Your kingdom is illusion
Your security, a dream

One day the sun will set for you
One day the light goes out
And as you gasp your final breath
Your hope becomes your doubt

It's just the same old story
And you know how it ends
The only chapters missing
Are how and where and when

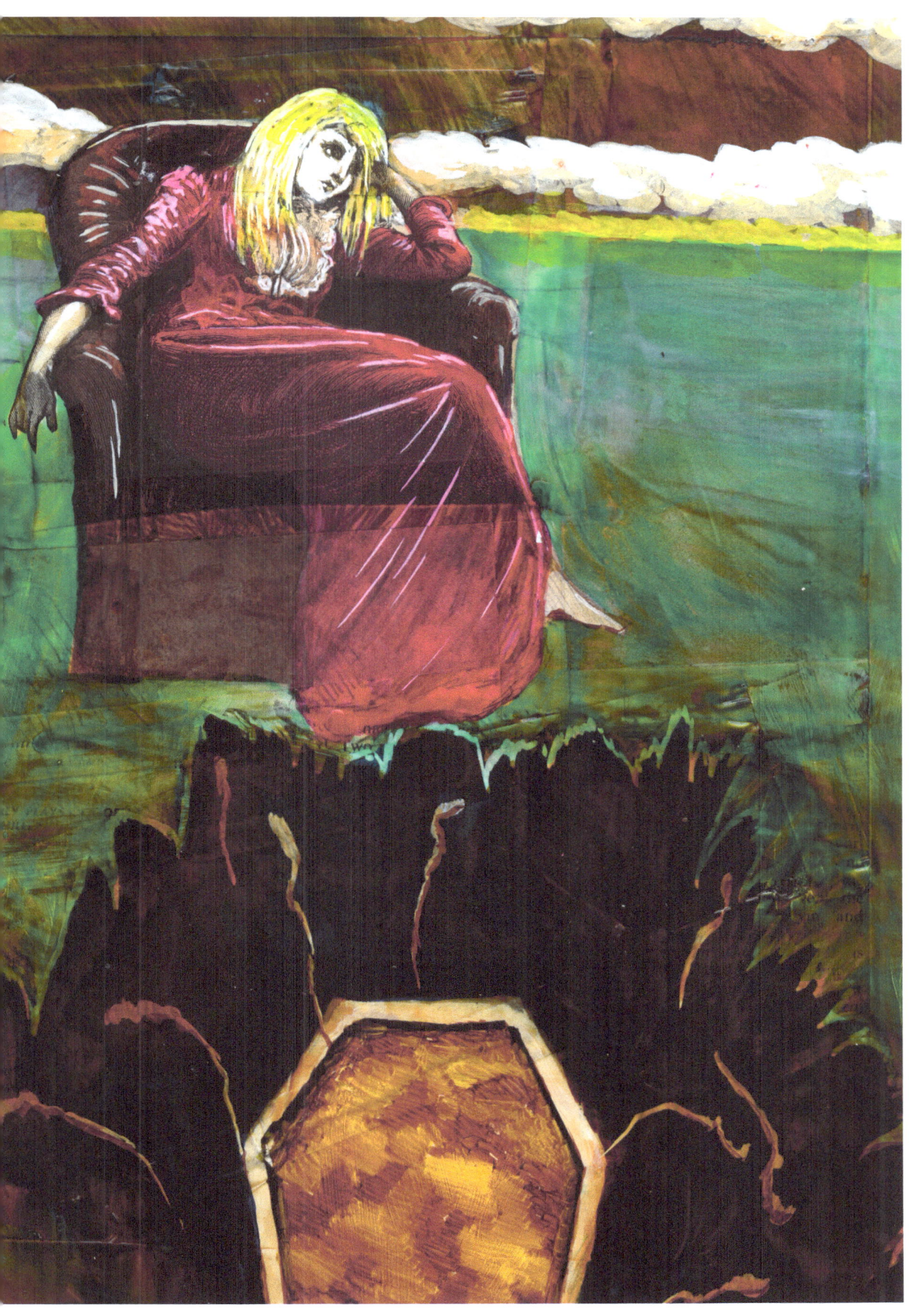

The angel of exits

One cut for every single lie
One slit for every tear
A slash for every severed tie
A gash for every fear

A nick for every lovely thing
You've ever ripped away
One wound for every ounce of pride
I lost in begging you to stay

An injury for every trust
Broken like my skin
The lesions left by acts of lust
That ruined
all that could have been

These long red lines
Will chart my fate
Like maps I cannot read
These deep red lines
Record my hate
And leave me here to bleed

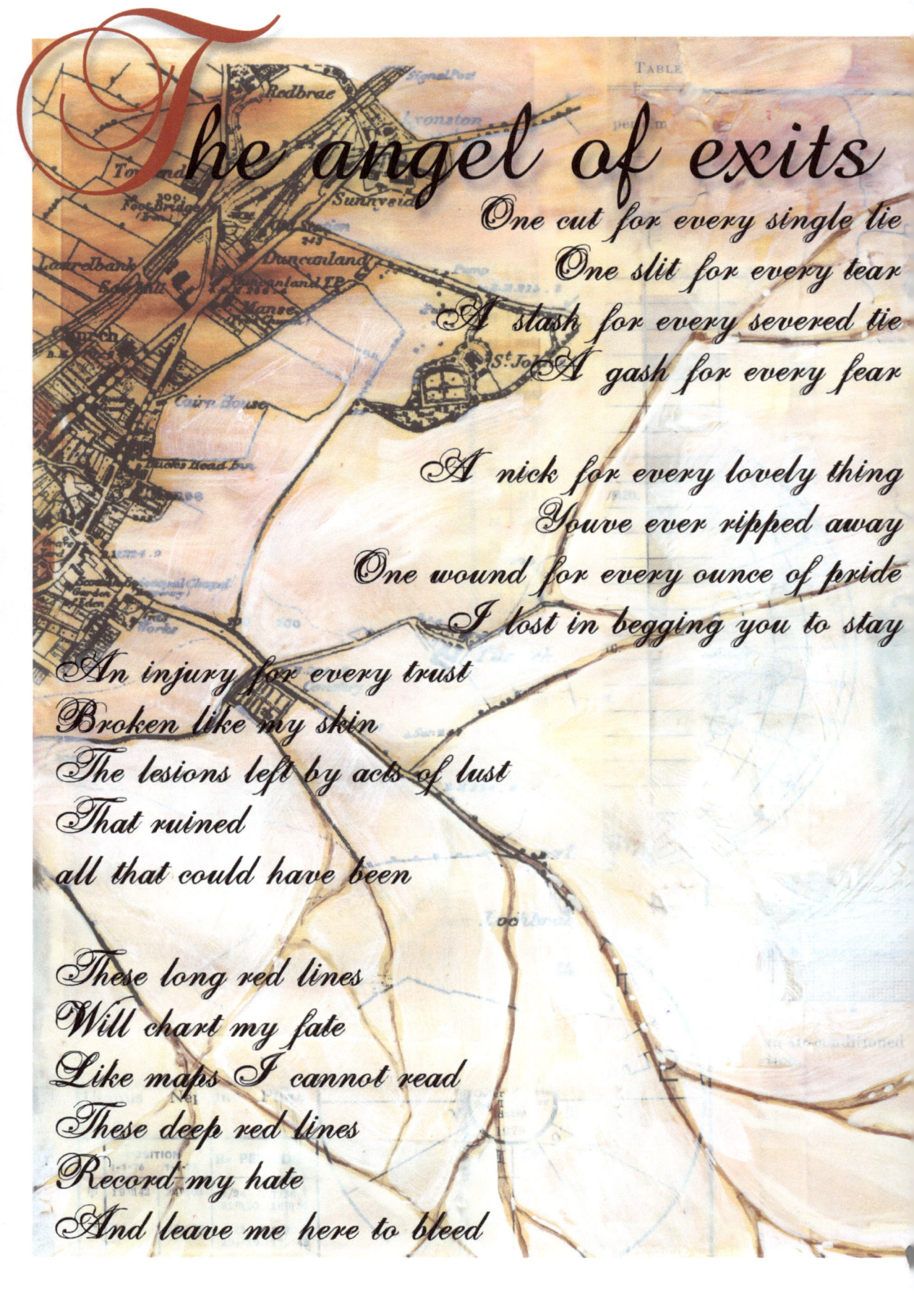

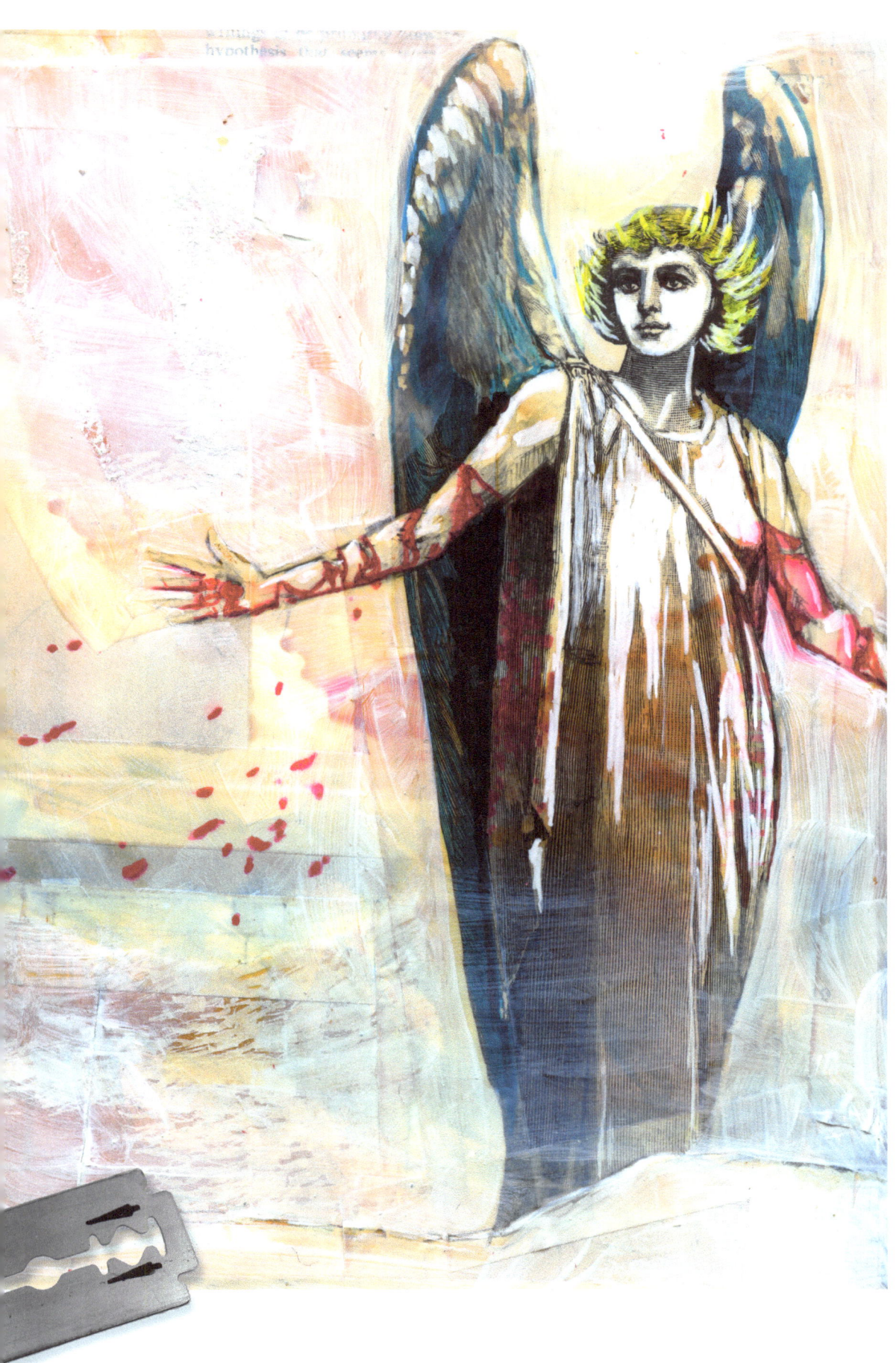

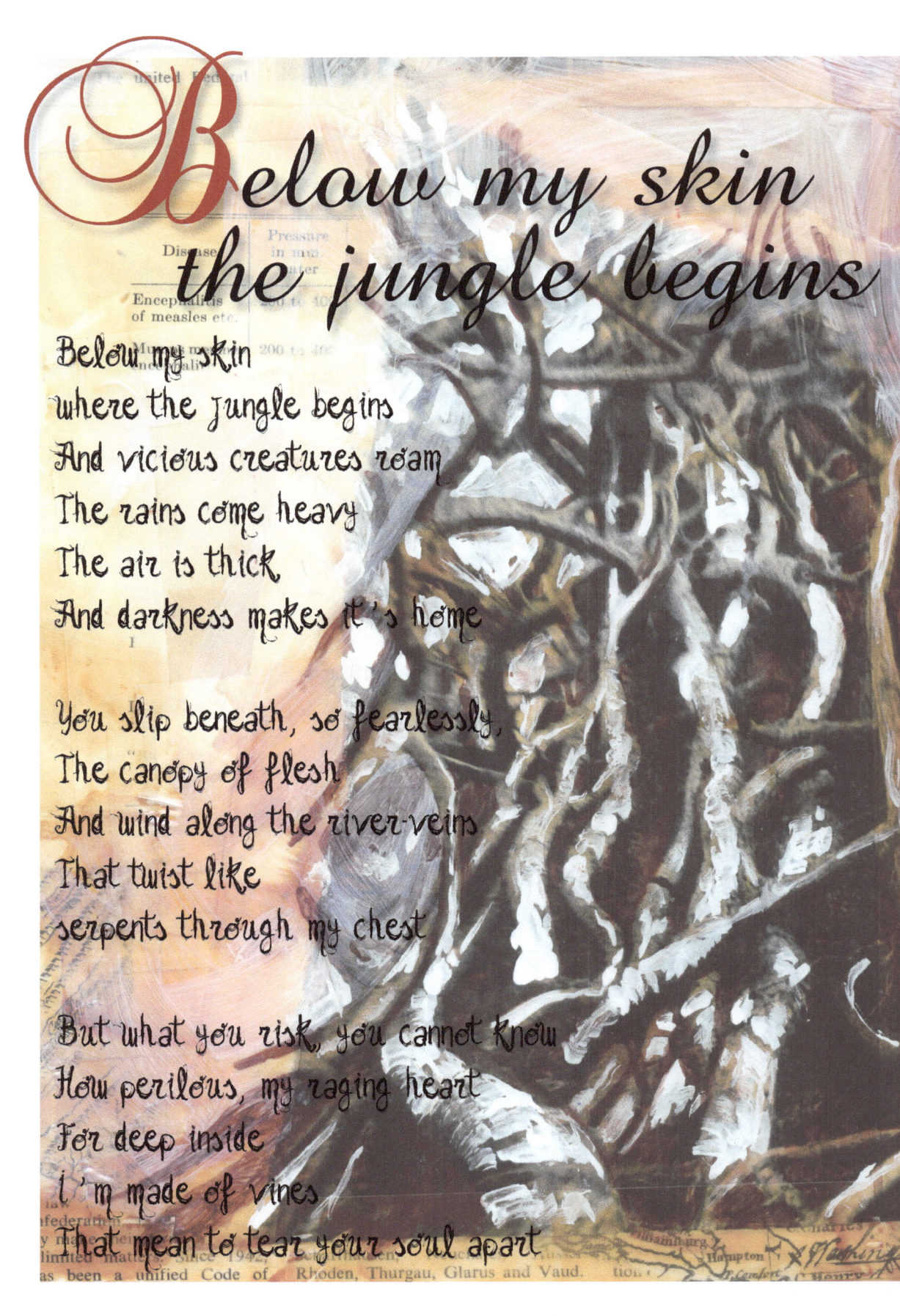

Below my skin the jungle begins

Below my skin
where the jungle begins
And vicious creatures roam
The rains come heavy
The air is thick,
And darkness makes it's home

You slip beneath, so fearlessly,
The canopy of flesh
And wind along the river-veins
That twist like
serpents through my chest

But what you risk, you cannot know
How perilous, my raging heart
For deep inside
I'm made of vines
That mean to tear your soul apart

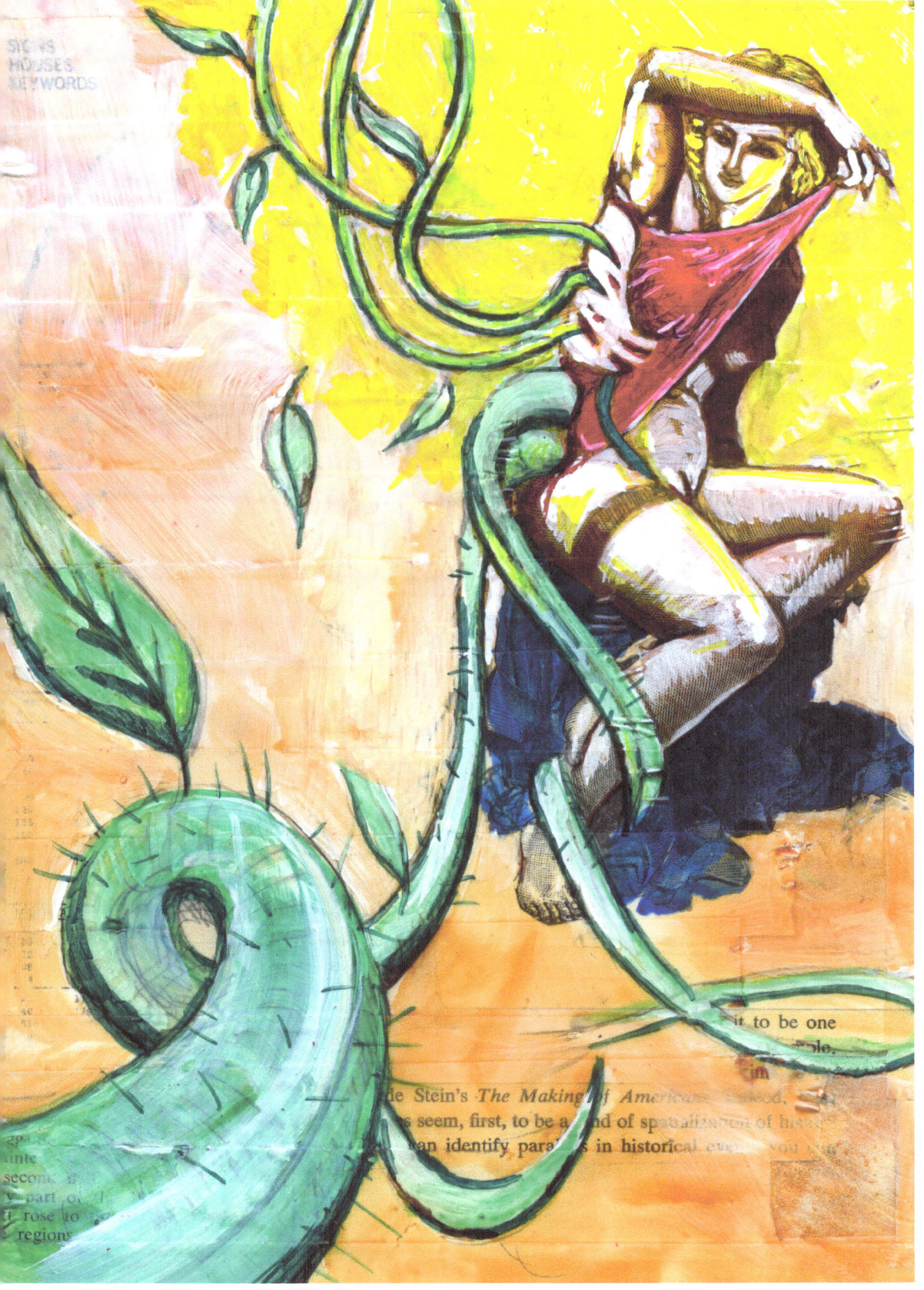

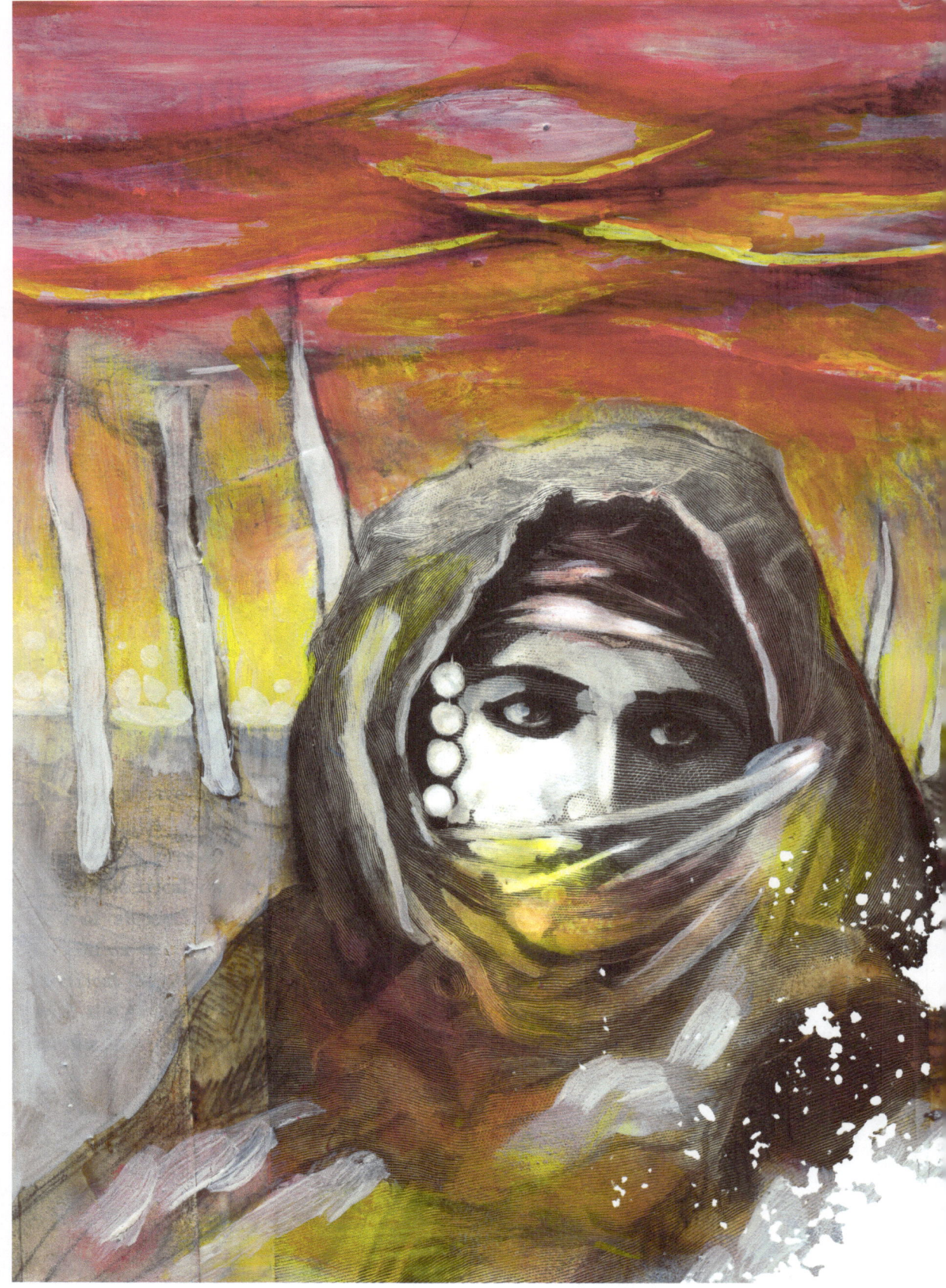

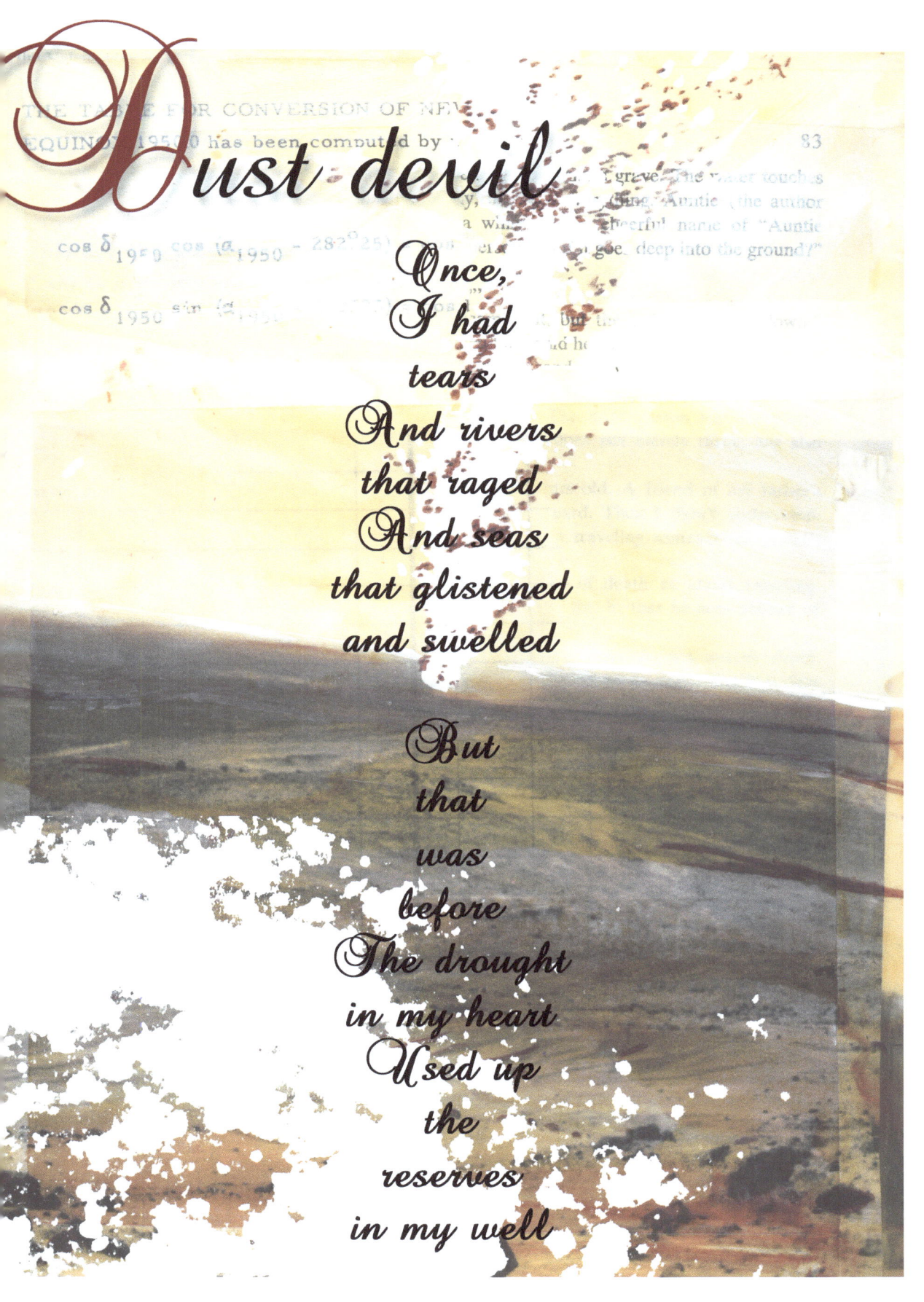

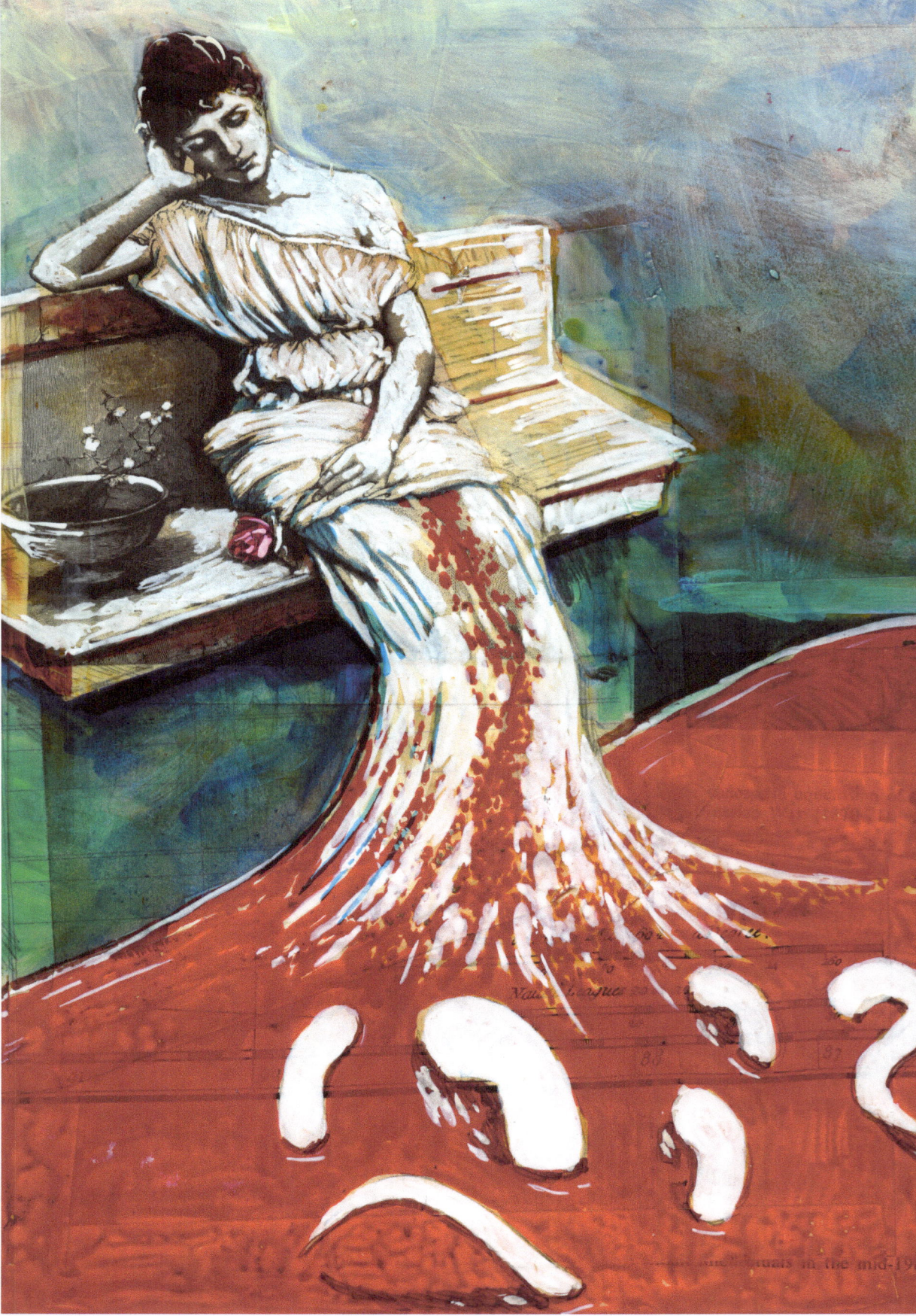

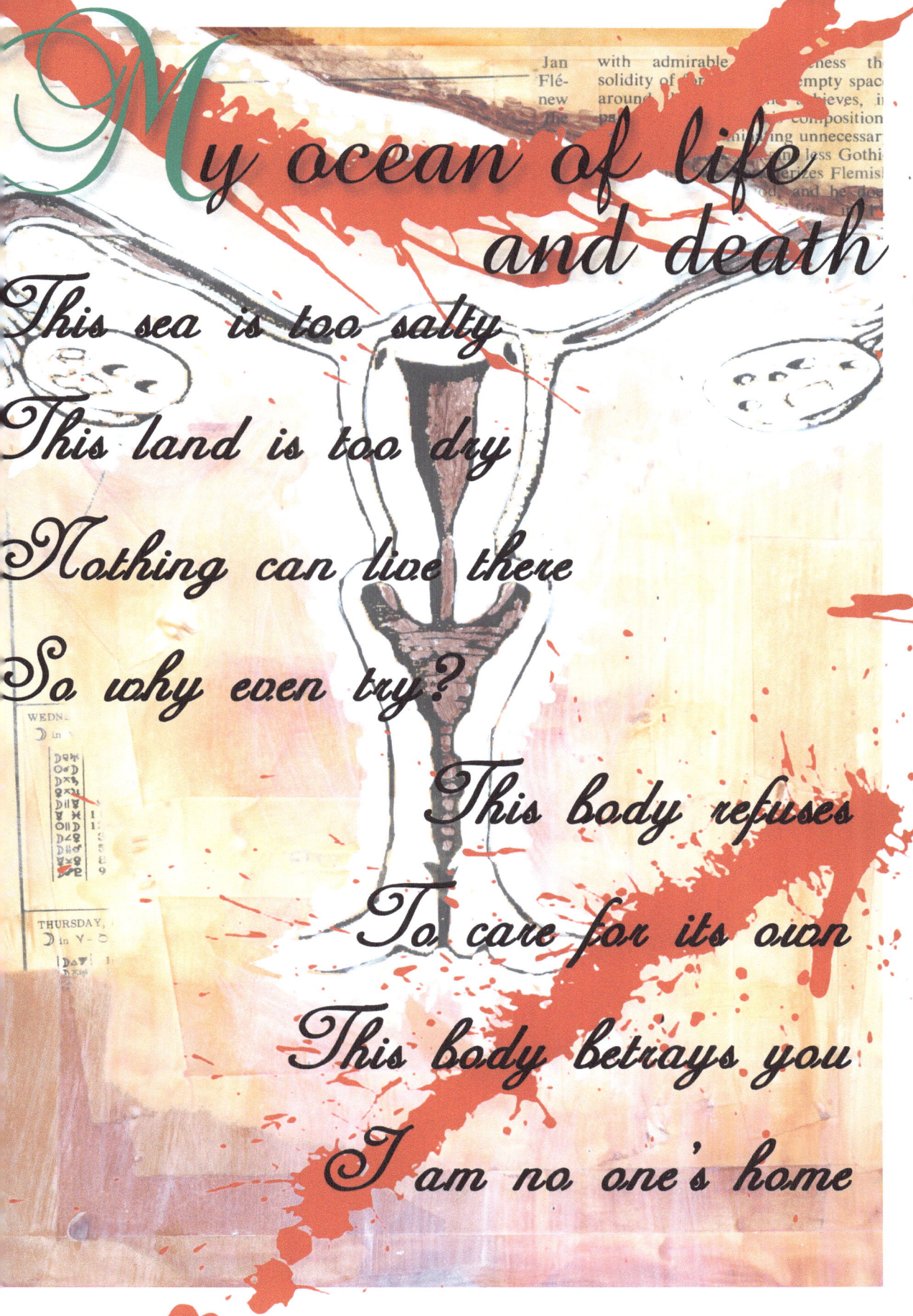

My ocean of life and death

This sea is too salty

This land is too dry

Nothing can live there

So why even try?

This body refuses

To care for its own

This body betrays you

I am no one's home

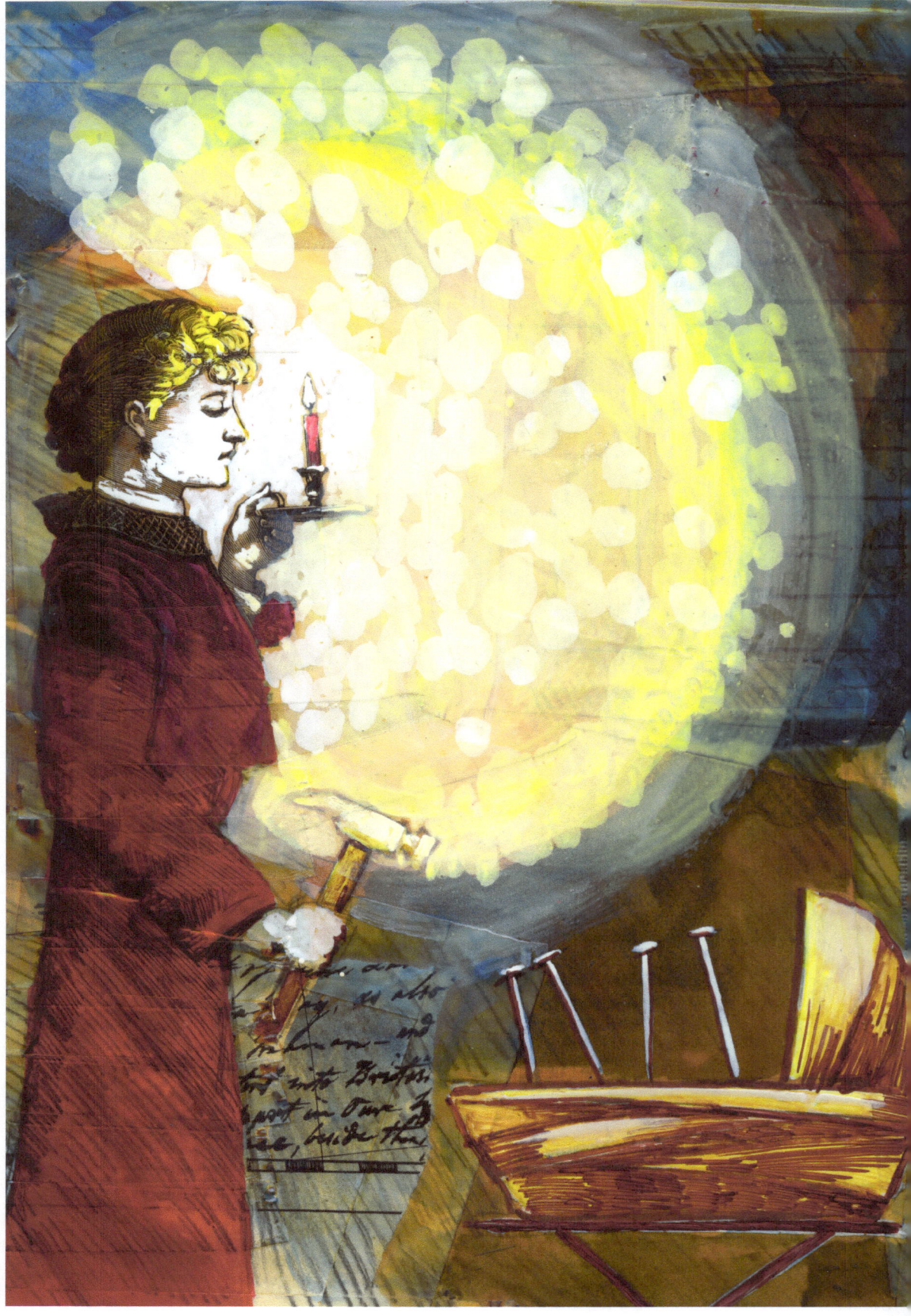

Nanny pounder

Hush, little baby
Don't make a sound
Nanny's gonna'
put you deep in the ground

    And if that ground
    should wash away
    Nanny's gonna'
    sink you in the bay

        And if that bay
        should swell and flood
        Nanny's gonna'
        put you in the mud

And if that mud
should ever dry
Nanny's gonna'
give you to the sky

    And if the sky
    should send you home
    Nanny's gonna'
    burn your tiny bones

        And if those bones
        won't crumble down
        Nanny's gonna'
        find another town

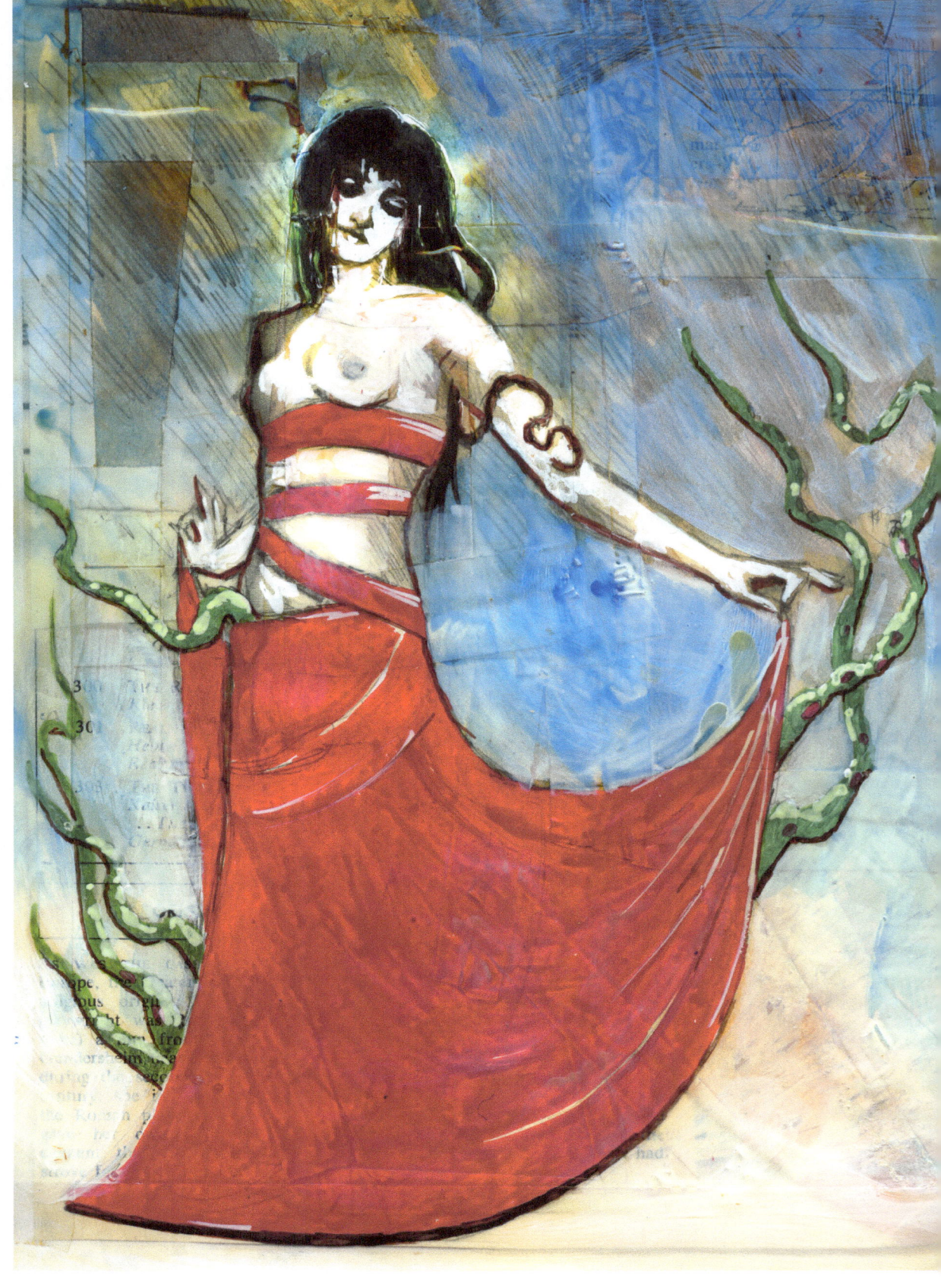

Our lady of perpetual twilight

The sun, it never sets on me
And never does it rise
It lingers in uncertainty
In tired, ashen skies

I am the saint to those who wait
Not sleeping or awake
And mother to the ones who cannot
Choose a path take

To those who fall between the hands
Of god, but not to Hell
To those who wish to cash it in
But have nothing to sell

To those who wish the answers
Might unfold before their eyes
I tell you now, my children,
Think me ignorant or wise

There is no absolute here
There is no wrong or right
The road you'd choose by light of day
You'd never take at night

For everything apparent
And all the things unseen
There's something terrible and lovely
About living in between

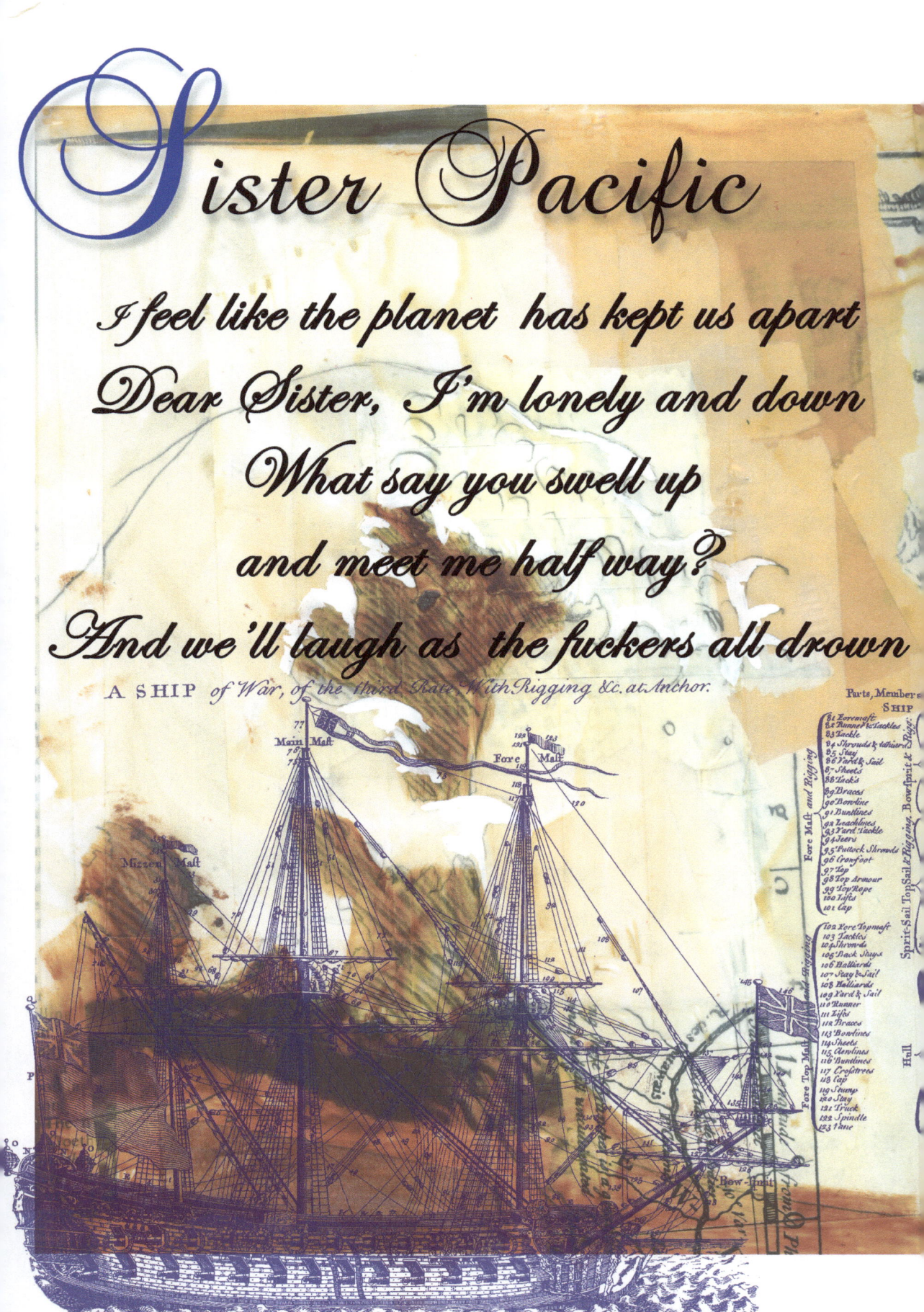

Sister Pacific

I feel like the planet has kept us apart
Dear Sister, I'm lonely and down
What say you swell up
and meet me half way?
And we'll laugh as the fuckers all drown

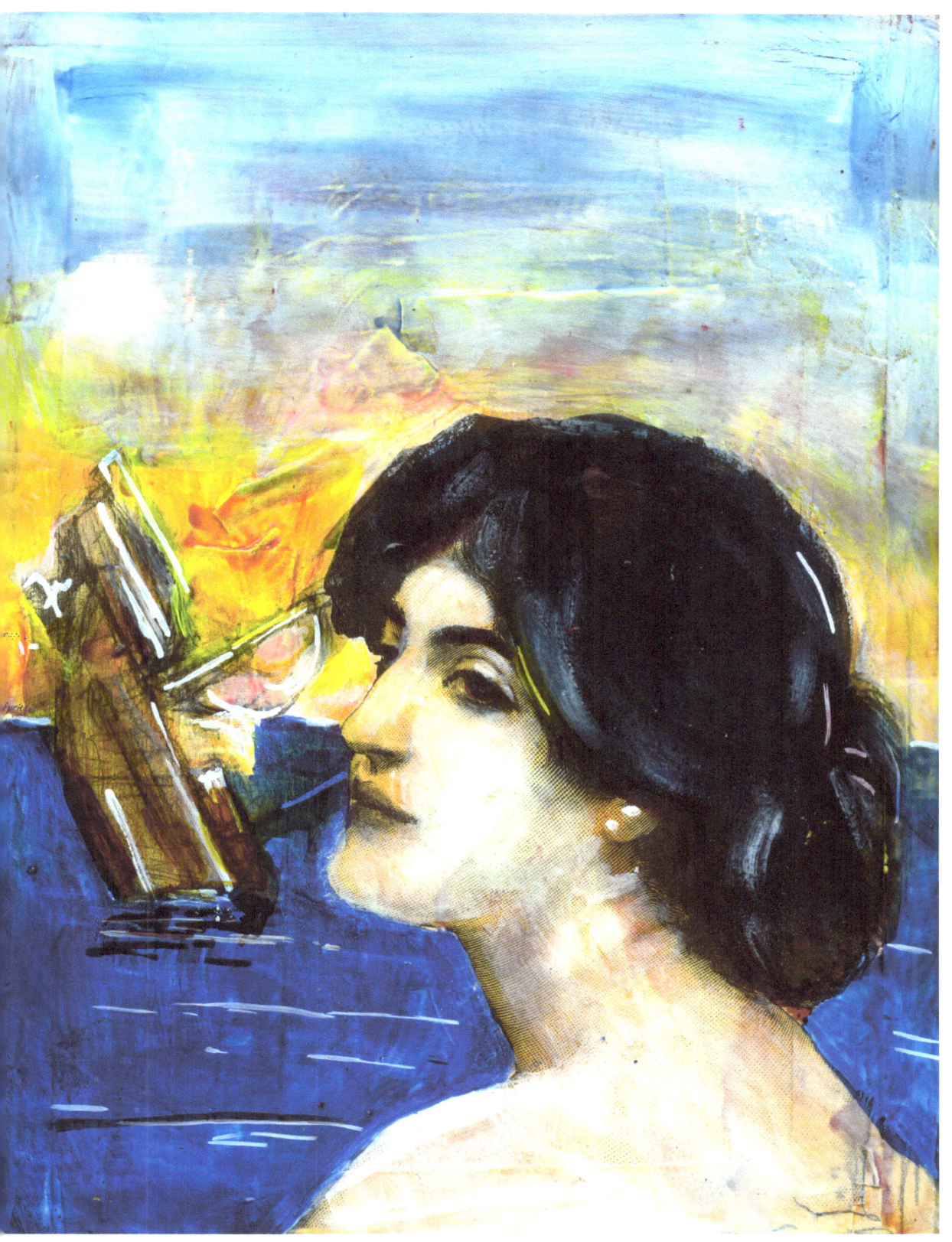

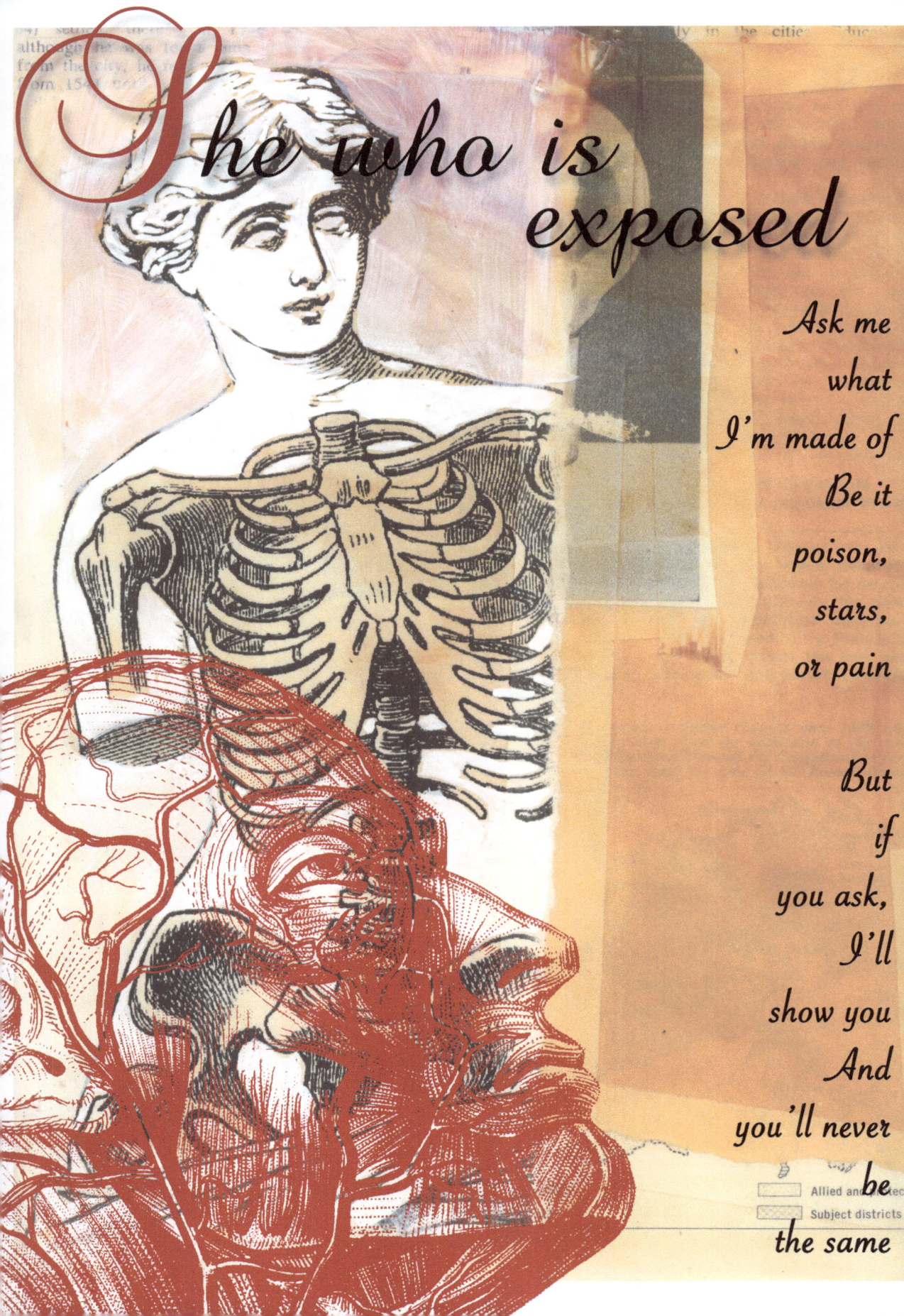

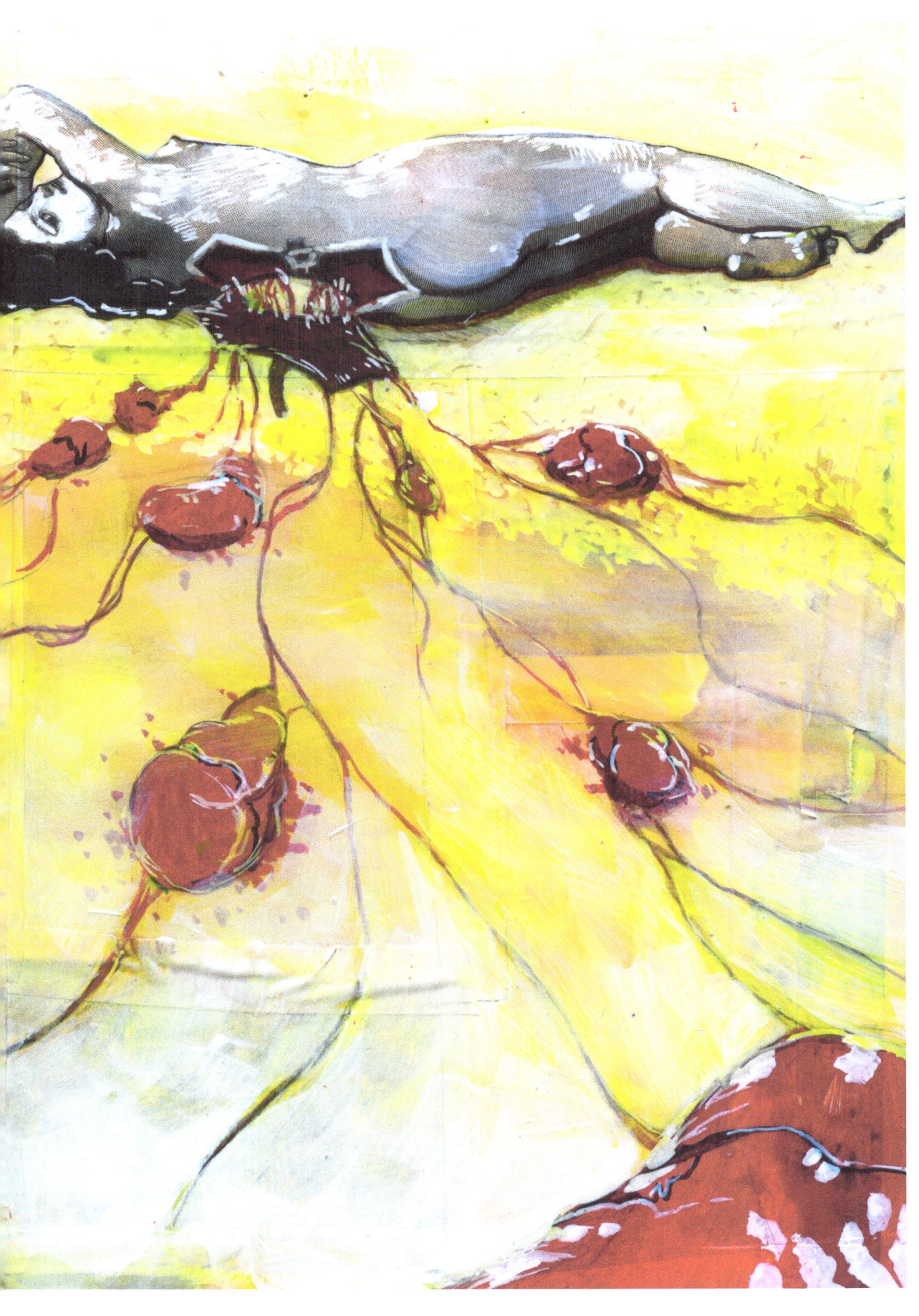

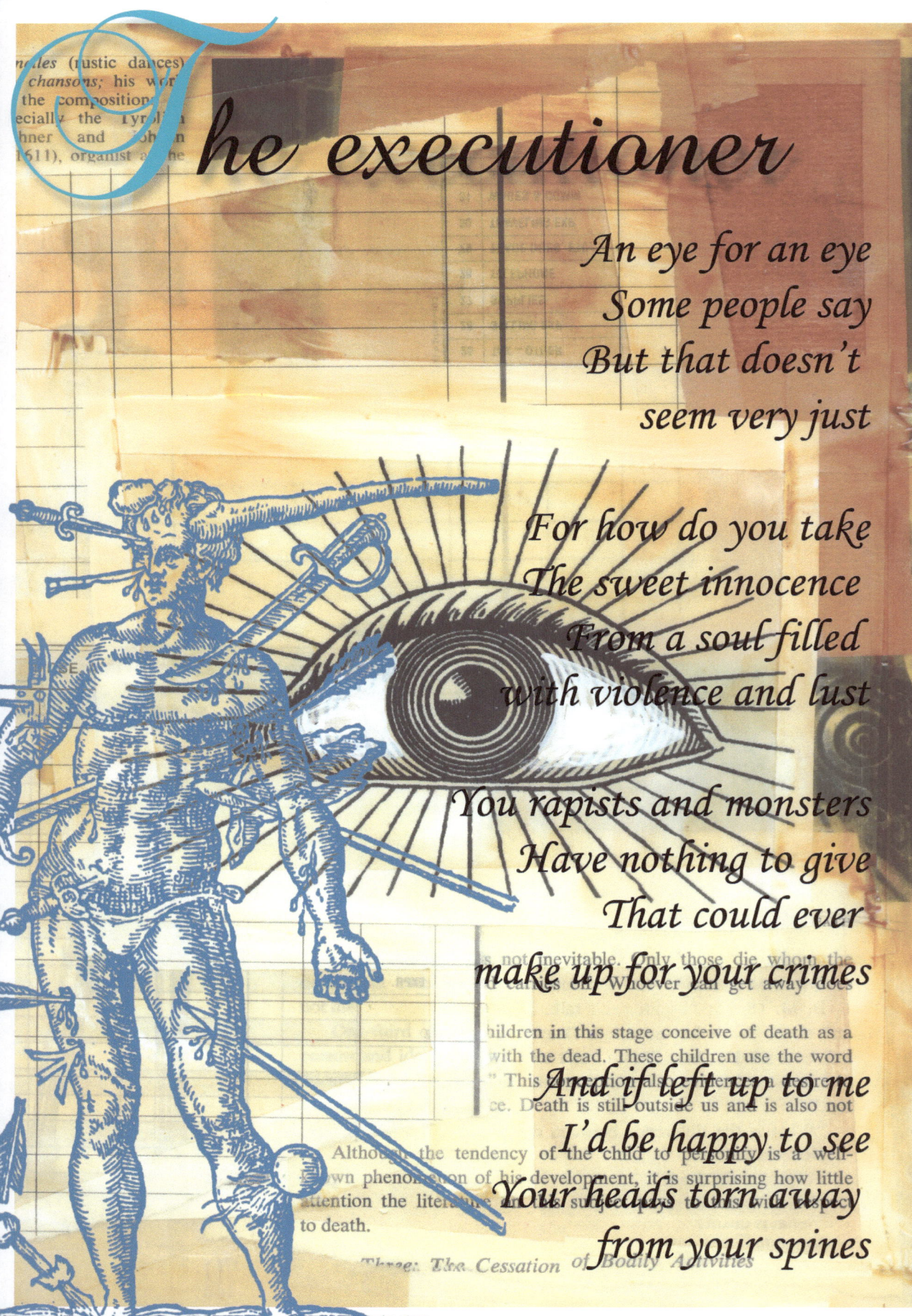

The executioner

An eye for an eye
Some people say
But that doesn't
seem very just

For how do you take
The sweet innocence
From a soul filled
with violence and lust

You rapists and monsters
Have nothing to give
That could ever
make up for your crimes

And if left up to me
I'd be happy to see
Your heads torn away
from your spines

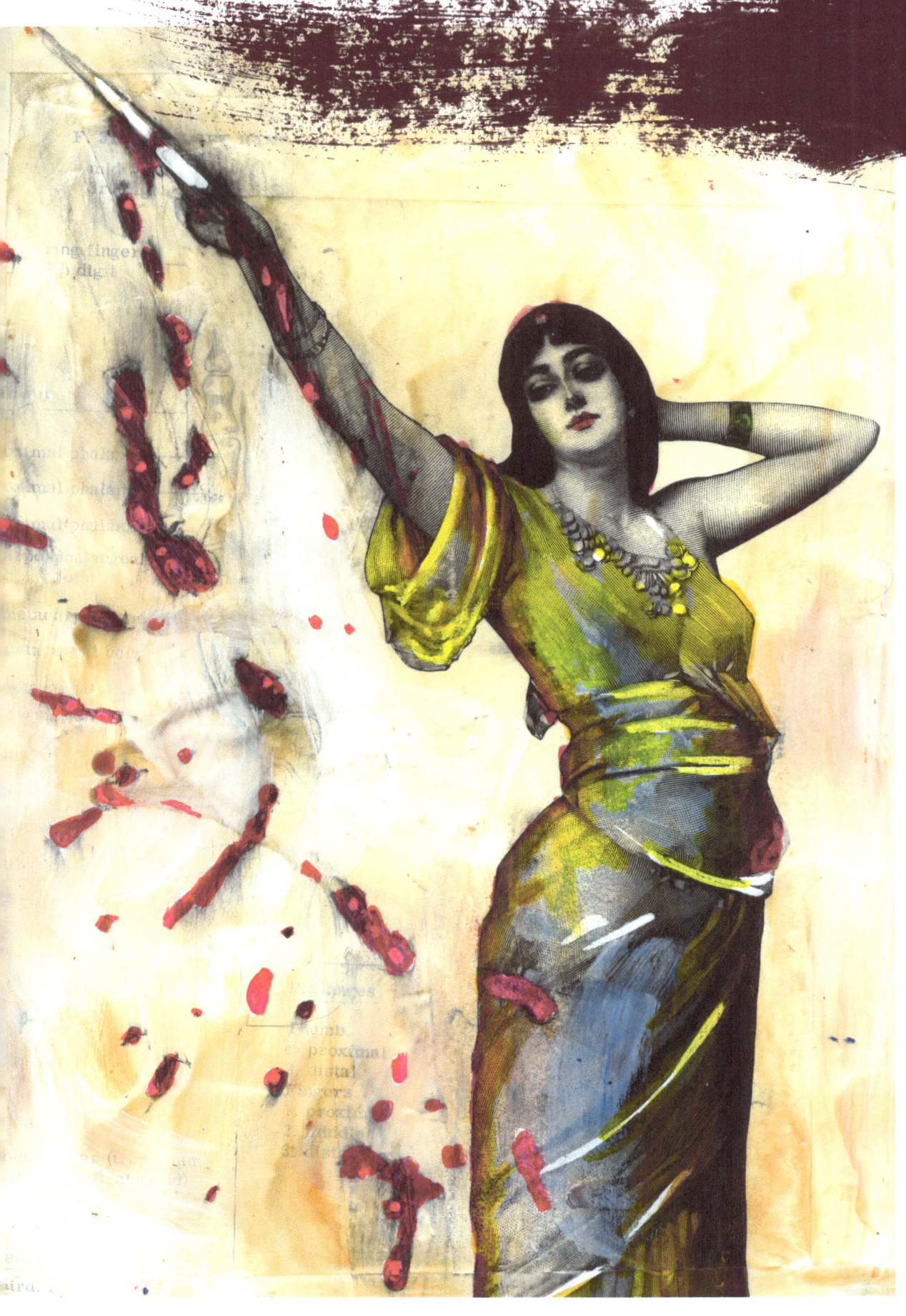

Stepping up

Something had to be done
Something had to be done
So I packed up the car
And loaded the gun

It was all bound to break
It was all bound to break
You can tell me I'm wrong
And I made a mistake

But I know what they took
And I know what I lost
And I know now they wished
They'd considered the cost

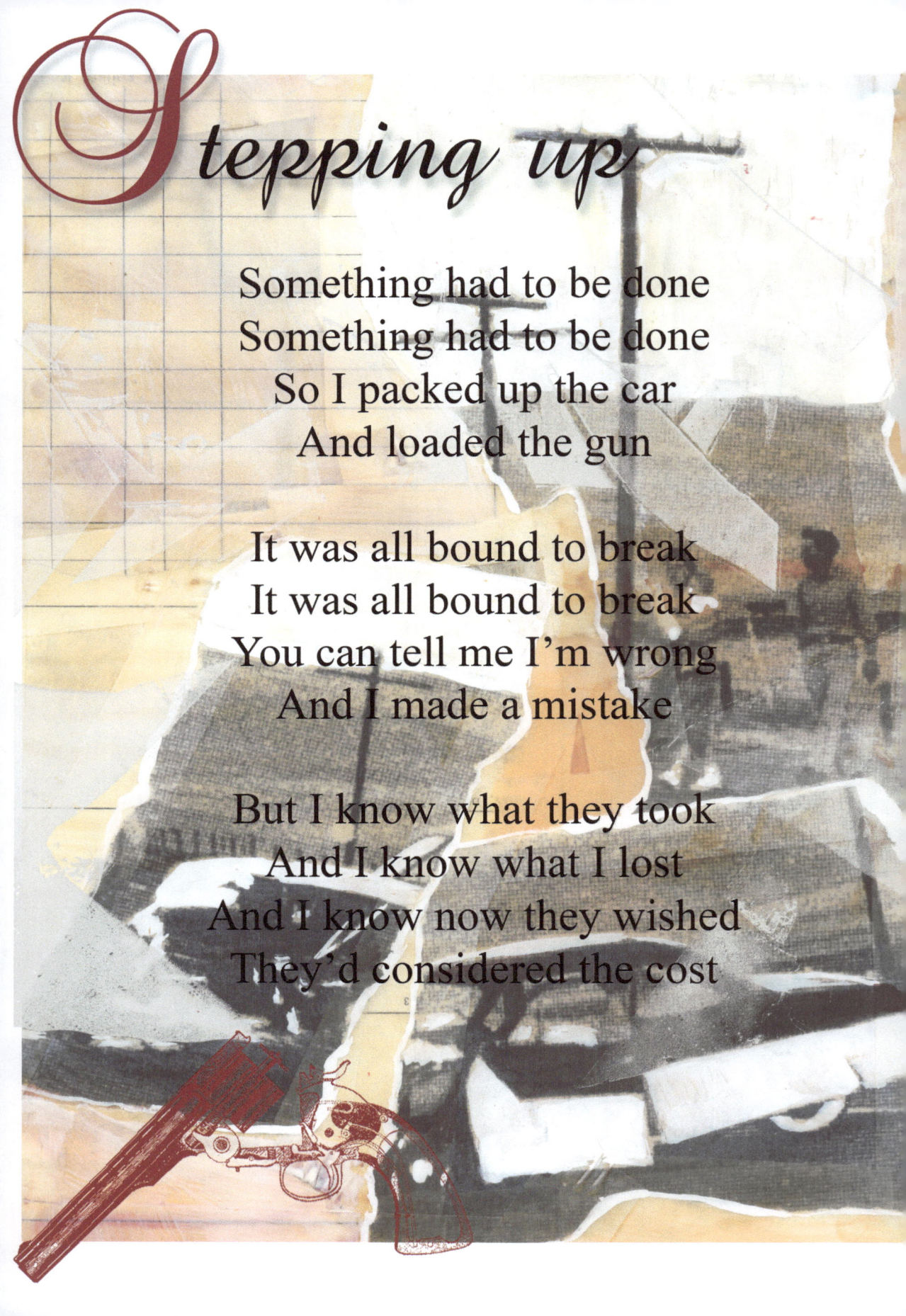

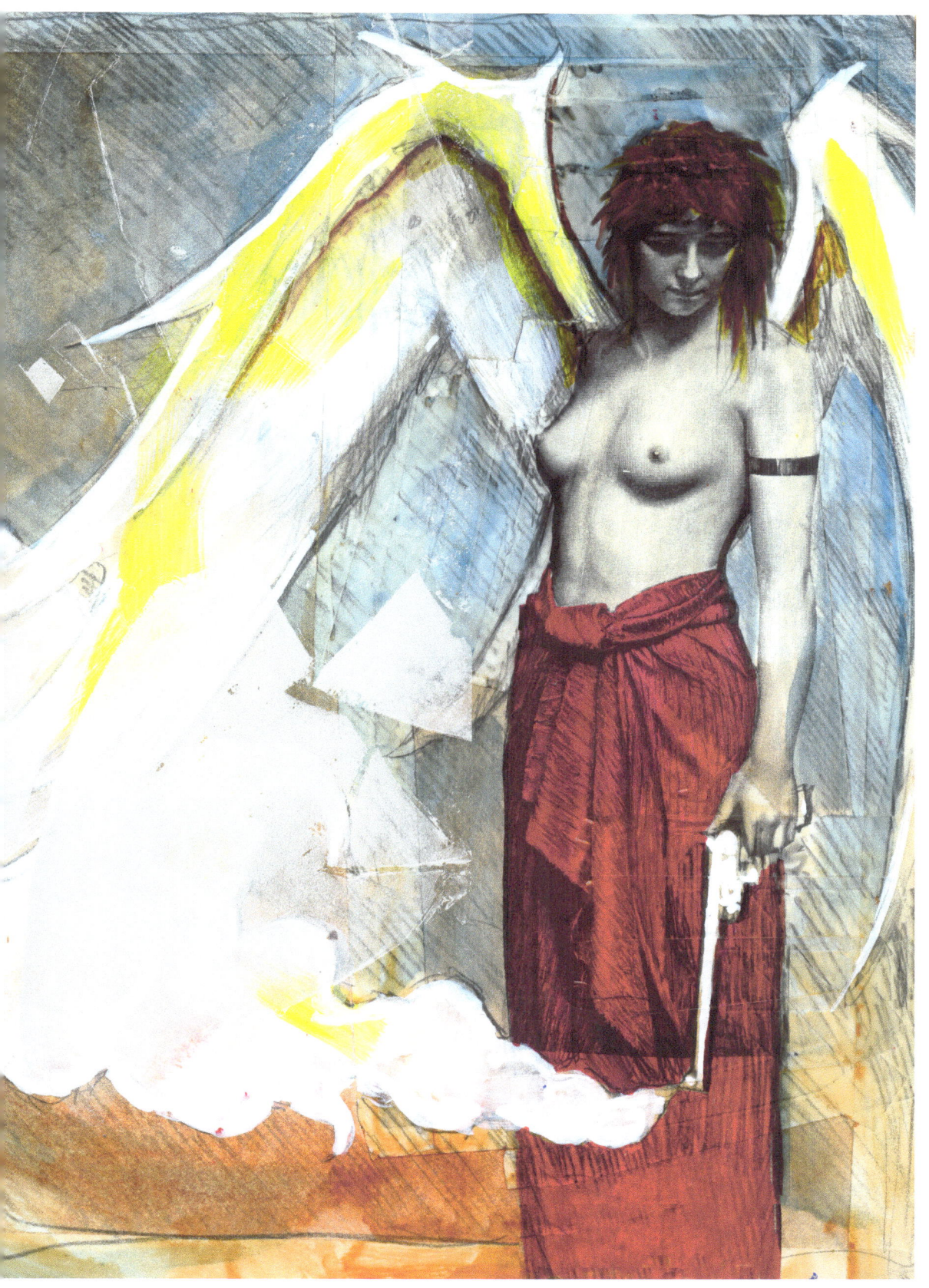

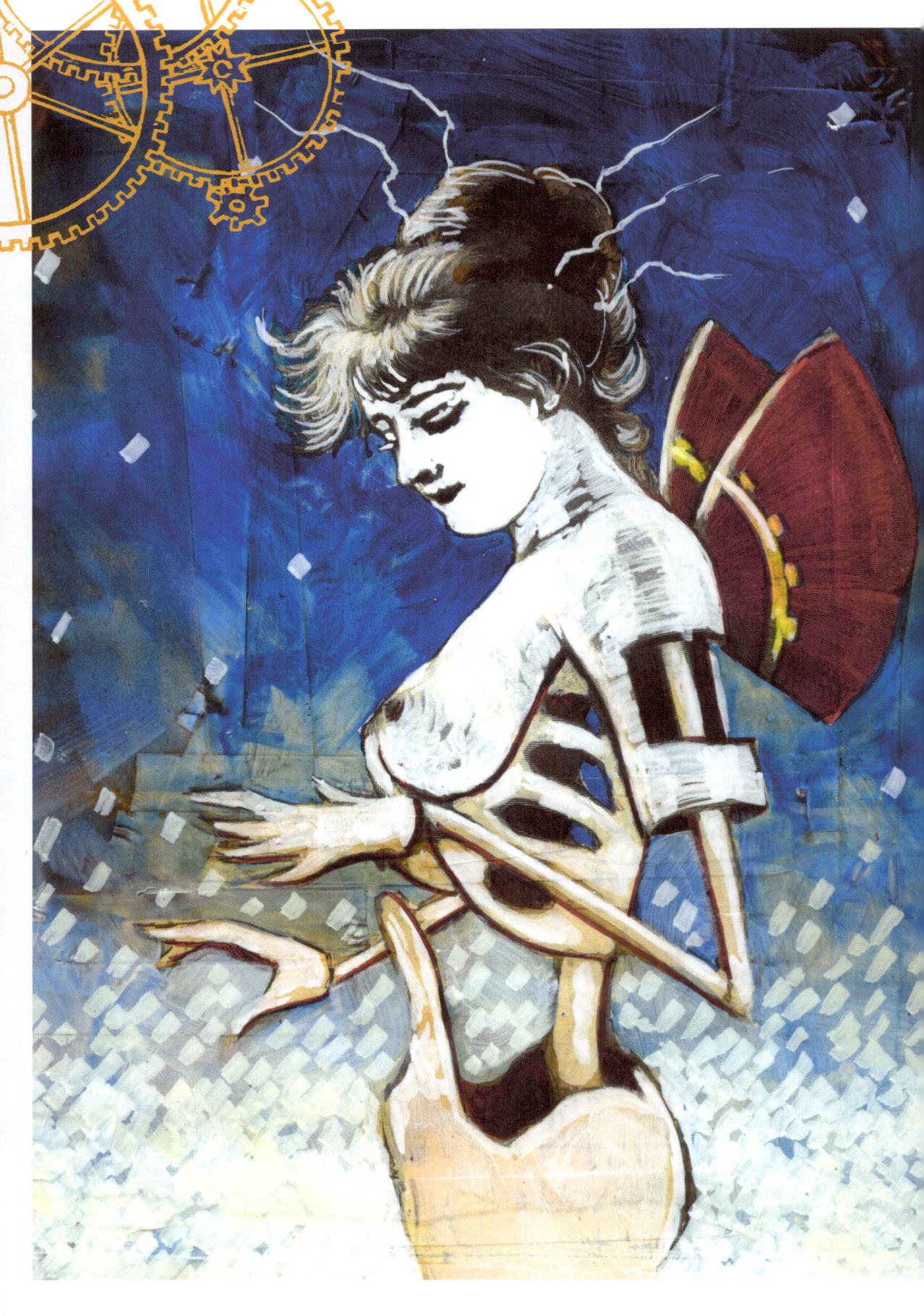

Queen of future myths

That little girls are always sweet
And wolves are most unkind
That serpents live to ruin men
And love will make you blind

That faeries bring you magic
And angels guide you home
That demons steal your spirit
And witches eat your bones

That loved ones will not leave you
And faith will see you through
The only thing I know for sure
Is that none of these are true

About the authors

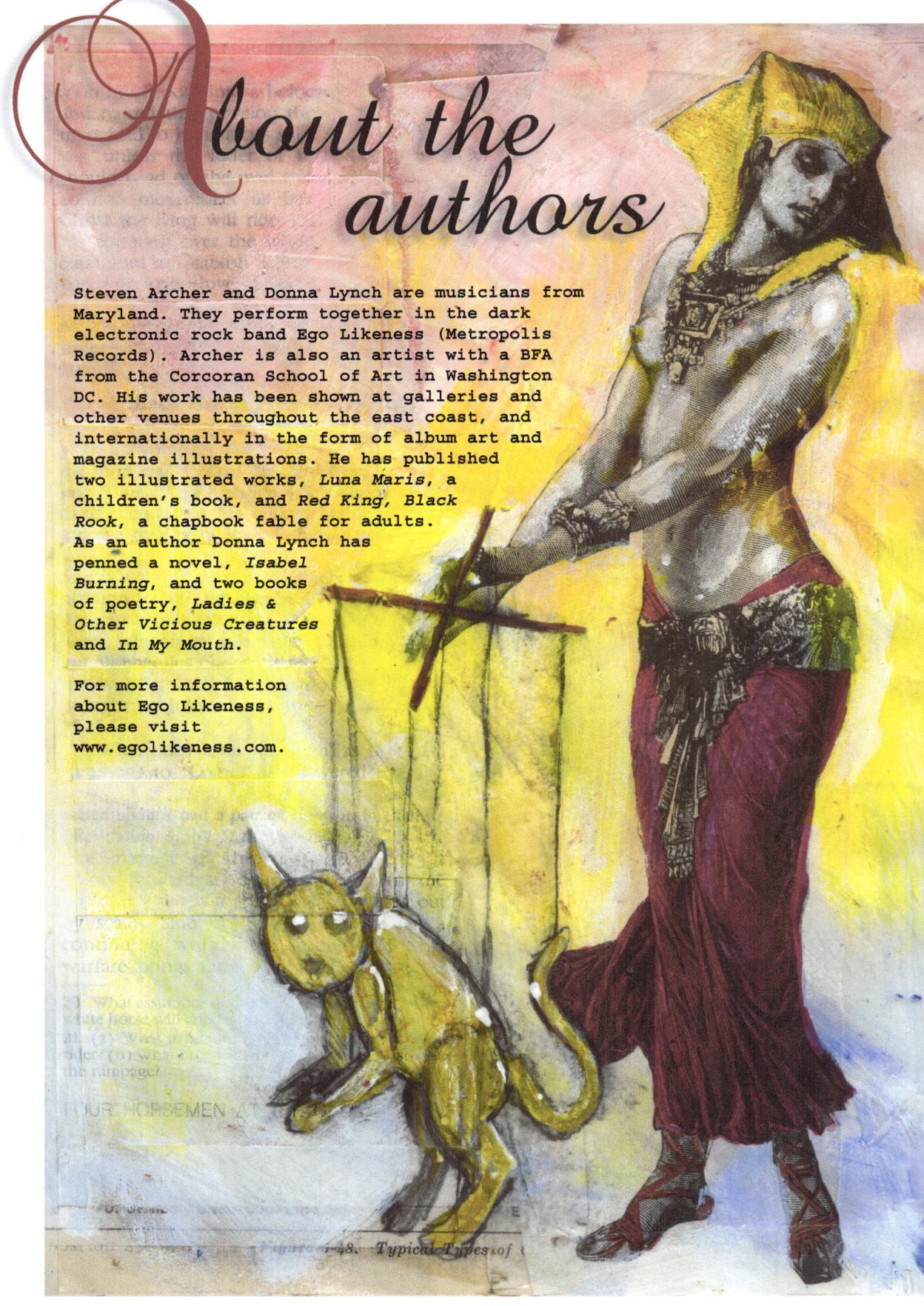

Steven Archer and Donna Lynch are musicians from Maryland. They perform together in the dark electronic rock band Ego Likeness (Metropolis Records). Archer is also an artist with a BFA from the Corcoran School of Art in Washington DC. His work has been shown at galleries and other venues throughout the east coast, and internationally in the form of album art and magazine illustrations. He has published two illustrated works, *Luna Maris*, a children's book, and *Red King, Black Rook*, a chapbook fable for adults. As an author Donna Lynch has penned a novel, *Isabel Burning*, and two books of poetry, *Ladies & Other Vicious Creatures* and *In My Mouth*.

For more information about Ego Likeness, please visit www.egolikeness.com.

www.ingramcontent.com/pod-product-compliance
Lightning Source LLC
Chambersburg PA
CBHW051207220526
45473CB00003B/943